Ted Tedrick, PhD
Editor

Older Adults with Developmental Disabilities and Leisure: Issues, Policy, and Practice

Older Adults
with Developmental Disabilities
and Leisure:
Issues, Policy, and Practice

T.M

Older Adults with Developmental Disabilities and Leisure: Issues, Policy, and Practice

Ted Tedrick, PhD
Editor

The Haworth Press, Inc.
New York • London

Older Adults with Developmental Disabilities and Leisure: Issues, Policy, and Practice has also been published as *Activities, Adaptation & Aging*, Volume 21, Number 3 1997.

Cover design by Donna M. Brooks.

The Haworth Press, Inc., 10 Alice Street, Binghamton, NY 13904-1580 USA

Library of Congress Cataloging-in-Publication Data

Older adults with developmental disabilities and leisure : issues, policy, and practice / Ted Tedrick, editor.
     p. cm.
     "Has also been published as Activites, adaptation & aging, Volume 21, number 3 1997"–T.p. verso
     Includes bibliographical references.
     ISBN 0-7890-0023-7
     1. Developmentally disabled aged–Recreation–United States. 2. Leisure–United States. 3. Developmentally disabled aged–Health and hygiene–United States. 4. Developmentally disabled aged–Services for–United States. I. Tedrick, Ted. II. Activities, adaptation & aging.
GV183.5.O53 1997   96-46303
796'.087'5–dc21   CIP

INDEXING & ABSTRACTING

Contributions to this publication are selectively indexed or abstracted in print, electronic, online, or CD-ROM version(s) of the reference tools and information services listed below. This list is current as of the copyright date of this publication. See the end of this section for additional notes.

- ***Abstracts in Social Gerontology: Current Literature on Aging***, National Council on the Aging, Library, 409 Third Street SW, 2nd Floor, Washington, DC 20024

- ***Abstracts of Research in Pastoral Care & Counseling***, Loyola College, 7135 Minstrel Way, Suite 101, Columbia, MD 21045

- ***AgeInfo CD-ROM***, Centre for Policy on Ageing, 25-31 Ironmonger Row, London EC1V 4QP, England

- ***AgeLine Database***, American Association of Retired Persons, 601 E Street, NW, Washington, DC 20049

- ***Alzheimer's Disease Education & Referral Center (ADEAR)***, Combined Health Information Database (CHID), P.O. Box 8250, Silver Spring, MD 20907-8250

- ***Brown University Geriatric Research Application Digest "Abstracts Section,"*** Brown University, Center for Gerontology & Health Research c/o Box G-B 235, Providence, RI 02912

- ***Cambridge Scientific Abstracts***, *Risk Abstracts,* Environmental Routenet (accessed via INTERNET), 7200 Wisconsin Avenue #601, Bethesda, MD 20814

- ***CINAHL (Cumulative Index to Nursing & Allied Health Literature), in print, also on CD-ROM from CD PLUS, EBSCO, and SilverPlatter, and online from CDP Online (formerly BRS), Data-Star, and PaperChase. (Support materials include Subject Heading List, Database Search Guide, and instructional video).*** CINAHL Information Systems, P. O. Box 871/1509 Wilson Terrace, Glendale, CA 91209-0871

(continued)

- *CNPIEC Reference Guide: Chinese National Directory of Foreign Periodicals,* P.O. Box 88, Beijing, Peoples Republic of China

- *Combined Health Information Database (CHID),* National Institutes of Health, 3 Information Way, Bethesda, MD 20892-3580

- *Communication Abstracts,* Temple University, 303 Annenberg Hall, Philadelphia, PA 19122

- *Family Studies Database (online and CD/ROM),* National Information Services Corporation, 306 East Baltimore Pike, 2nd Floor, Media, PA 19063

- *Health Care Literature Information Network/HECLINET,* Technische Universitat Berlin/Dokumentation Krankenhauswesen, Sekr. A42, Strasse des 17. Juni 135, D 10623 Berlin, Germany

- *Human Resources Abstracts (HRA),* Sage Publications, Inc., 2455 Teller Road, Newbury Park, CA 91320

  IBZ International Bibliography of Periodical Literature, Zeller Verlag GmbH & Co., P.O.B. 1949, D-49009 Osnabruck, Germany

- *INTERNET ACCESS (& additional networks) Bulletin Board for Libraries ("BUBL"), coverage of information resources on INTERNET, JANET, and other networks.*
  - JANET X.29: UK.AC.BATH.BUBL or 0006012101300
  - TELNET: BUBL.BATH.AC.UK or 138.38.32.45 login 'bubl'
  - Gopher: BUBL.BATH.AC.UK (138.32.32.45). Port 7070
  - World Wide Web: http: / / www.bubl.bath.ac.uk./BUBL/ home.html
  - NISSWAIS: telnetniss.ac. uk (for the NISS gateway)
  The Andersonian Library, Curran Building, 101 St. James Road, Glasgow G4 ONS, Scotland

- *Leisure, Recreation and Tourism Abstracts, c/o CAB International/CAB ACCESS . . . available in print, diskettes updated weekly, and on INTERNET. Providing full bibliographic listings, author affiliation, augmented keyword searching,* CAB International, P.O. Box 100, Wallingford Oxon OX10 8DE, United Kingdom

(continued)

- *Mental Health Abstracts (online through DIALOG),* IFI/Plenum Data Company, 3202 Kirkwood Highway, Wilmington, DE 19808

- *National Clearinghouse for Primary Care Information (NCPCI),* 8201 Greensboro Drive, Suite 600, McLean, VA 22102

- *New Literature on Old Age,* Centre for Policy on Ageing, 25-31 Ironmonger Row, London EC1V 3QP, England

- *OT BibSys,* American Occupational Therapy Foundation, P. O. Box 31220, Rockville, MD 20824-1220

- *Psychological Abstracts (PsycINFO),* American Psychological Association, P. O. Box 91600, Washington, DC 20090-1600

- *Referativnyi Zhurnal (Abstracts Journal of the Institute of Scientific Information of the Republic of Russia),* The Institute of Scientific Information, Baltijskaja ul., 14, Moscow A-219, Republic of Russia

- *Social Planning/Policy & Development Abstracts (SOPODA),* Sociological Abstracts, Inc., P. O. Box 22206, San Diego, CA 92192-0206

- *Social Work Abstracts,* National Association of Social Workers, 750 First Street NW, 8th Floor, Washington, DC 20002

- *Sociological Abstracts (SA),* Sociological Abstracts, Inc., P. O. Box 22206, San Diego, CA 92192-0206

- *Special Educational Needs Abstracts,* Carfax Information Systems, P. O. Box 25, Abingdon, Oxfordshire OX14 3UE, United Kingdom

- *Sport Database/Discus,* Sport Information Resource Center, 1600 James Naismith Drive, Suite 107, Gloucester, Ontario K1B 5N4, Canada

(continued)

SPECIAL BIBLIOGRAPHIC NOTES

related to special journal issues (separates)
and indexing/abstracting

☐ indexing/abstracting services in this list will also cover material in any "separate" that is co-published simultaneously with Haworth's special thematic journal issue or DocuSerial. Indexing/abstracting usually covers material at the article/chapter level.

☐ monographic co-editions are intended for either non-subscribers or libraries which intend to purchase a second copy for their circulating collections.

☐ monographic co-editions are reported to all jobbers/wholesalers/approval plans. The source journal is listed as the "series" to assist the prevention of duplicate purchasing in the same manner utilized for books-in-series.

☐ to facilitate user/access services all indexing/abstracting services are encouraged to utilize the co-indexing entry note indicated at the bottom of the first page of each article/chapter/contribution.

☐ this is intended to assist a library user of any reference tool (whether print, electronic, online, or CD-ROM) to locate the monographic version if the library has purchased this version but not a subscription to the source journal.

☐ individual articles/chapters in any Haworth publication are also available through the Haworth Document Delivery Services (HDDS).

Older Adults with Developmental Disabilities and Leisure: Issues, Policy, and Practice

CONTENTS

∞ ALL HAWORTH BOOKS AND JOURNALS
ARE PRINTED ON CERTIFIED
ACID-FREE PAPER

ABOUT THE EDITOR

Ted Tedrick, PhD, is Professor in the Department of Sports Management and Leisure Studies at Temple University in Philadelphia. The co-author of *Activity Experiences and Programming Within Long-Term Care,* and *Leisure and Aging: Ulyssean Living in Later Life*, he is an Associate Editor and frequent contributor to *Activities, Adaptation & Aging* and recently completed a manual for caregivers and staff assisting older adults with developmental disabilities. His interest in leisure and aging has been pursued in the classroom, in workshops and seminars for professionals, and as a practitioner. Professor Tedrick serves on the Boards of the Leisure and Aging Society and the Mayor's Commission on Services to the Aging in Philadelphia.

Introduction

Those with an interest in the aging of adults with mental retardation/developmental disabilities (MR/DD), are well aware of the growth of this sub-population. Not only have services had to expand or be created to meet this need, but professionals and researchers have responded through books, monographs, and journals. As Sutton (chapter five) notes, "The past decade has seen an explosion in published research and practice approaches."

An element of quality of life particularly relevant to those who are aging is the degree to which leisure experiences can provide meaning, time structure, and satisfaction to daily living. Indeed, as Hawkins reports (chapter two), leisure participation is related to life satisfaction for adults with mental retardation. Thus, issues surrounding leisure for older adults with MR/DD including: knowledge of current patterns and desirability of change, the degree to which community integration is appropriate for all, and how leisure education programs can be implemented, serve as the focus for this monograph.

Jean Keller in 1991 edited *Activities with Developmentally Disabled Elderly and Older Adults* (Keller, 1991) and many of the same concerns, issues, and problems remain with us currently, although progress has been made in recognizing the needs of this group. Much programming creativity has been reported, particularly with an emphasis on inclusion or community integration, or "community membership" as Barret and Clements refer to it in this work. We felt it was time to revisit issues introduced in that earlier volume and to look at the future as well, thus the authors within this book were asked to address issues within their area of expertise

---

[Haworth co-indexing entry note]: "Introduction." Tedrick, Ted. Co-published simultaneously in *Activities, Adaptation & Aging* (The Haworth Press, Inc.) Vol. 21, No. 3, 1997, pp. 1-6; and: *Older Adults with Developmental Disabilities and Leisure: Issues, Policy, and Practice* (ed: Ted Tedrick) The Haworth Press, Inc., 1997, pp. 1-6. Single or multiple copies of this article are available for a fee from The Haworth Document Delivery Service [1-800-342-9678, 9:00 a.m. - 5:00 p.m. (EST). E-mail address: getinfo@haworth.com].

1

pertinent to the broad scope of leisure in the lives of aging persons with developmental disabilities.

The lead article by Boyd serves two purposes: to introduce the reader by way of review to knowledge about the population of aging adults with developmental disabilities and to broach issues or concerns dealing with leisure and retirement which are examined by other authors who follow. Three central themes dominate the discussion: inactivity, especially in physical pursuits during later life leads to problems; life satisfaction for adults with developmental disabilities is correlated with leisure participation; and the leisure profile for most of this group centers on rather passive, sedentary time-fillers which further emphasizes the importance of the first theme. Decision-making is addressed; not only is there a need for staff to educate those who may have had little practice with selecting among options, but ethical dilemmas may ensue once choice is given to empowered clients. How do staff react when personal choice leads to poor health habits or inactive lifestyles? Boyd highlights the demography of aging adults with developmental disabilities and then shifts to the areas of functional skill levels and the physical and psycho-social domains. Leisure patterns of this group are reviewed followed by a discussion of what retirement might mean and problems associated with it relating to the mental retardation/developmental disability system. Community integration, including models which have been successful, is the topic concluding the chapter.

As suggested above, increased physical activity has been suggested for adults with developmental disabilities. The papers by Hawkins and Frizzell support that recommendation and offer guidelines in establishing fitness programming. Using a three-year longitudinal study as a base, Hawkins reports that gender and nature of retardation, Down syndrome vs. non-Down syndrome, are responsible for differences in areas of physical and cognitive functioning. Age was found to be negatively correlated with both life satisfaction and leisure participation. Stress is a factor in the lives of many aging adults with developmental disabilities, although Hawkins notes that it may not be considered by staff. Frizzell offers specific considerations or guides for establishing fitness programs. There is a need for certified personnel who not only are competent in instructing exercise, but who also possess knowledge about aging and mental retardation/developmental disabilities–such a combination is a rare find. There is a need, according to Frizzell, to introduce lifetime activities or sports such as biking, tennis, or swimming to persons with developmental disabilities and this should be done prior to or in the early adult years. Most of the current older cohort of adults with mental retardation have not been exposed to this type of activity. Frizzell offers examples of specific exercise programs, giant beach ball and exer-band exercises, giving goals and keys for maximum participation such as staff using constant reinforcement and enthusiasm. The focus here is for personnel wishing to begin a fitness program.

The arts provide a vehicle for fulfilling many needs of older adults–those with and without disabilities as Barret and Clements discuss in chapter four. Inclusion and community membership are two important themes as the authors detail specific arts programs designed for adults with and without disabilities. We learn that many benefits accrue: peer interaction, flexible thinking, self-expression, and improved mental health when adults indulge in art programming. Using a proven model, the Arts/Fitness Quality of Life Activities Program, the authors detail how careful planning and sequencing can achieve desired objectives. One successful effort called "Important People" introduced photography and cultural history to older adults (some with, others without developmental disabilities) through preparatory slide shows to visitation of a photographic exhibit to the last phase where participants took their own photographs and shared them with the group. Community membership was evident in the fullest sense.

Sutton, in chapter five, traces the impact of deinstitutionalization in the 1970s upon today's older cohort of persons with MR/DD. By way of survey research conducted to gather basic descriptive information about this population such as health, activities, and social opportunities and through explanation of model programs which were developed by Sutton and her colleagues at the University of Akron, she provides a historical review and brings us to current issues needing resolution. Among these are an understanding of the role of retirement in the lives of those adults with developmental disabilities who elect such an option and how the MR system can accommodate retirement when habilitation, training goals, and some type of employment have been the major thrusts for persons within the system throughout their adult years. We learn that many potential retirees do not embrace the concept, perhaps due to years of habit, or friendships made at the work setting, or fear of giving up even nominal wages which have been earned at sheltered workshops. Sutton concludes that the system must be flexible–allowing work or phase-down for those desiring such options and meaningful retirement for those electing it. Ohio, for example, includes retirement in its regulations addressing program needs of adults with developmental disabilities. Pre-retirement planning is most often lacking for this group and a model curriculum, "Person-Centered Planning for Later Life" is highlighted.

The paper by Wilhite and Sheldon raises a fundamental consideration, to what degree are consumers with developmental disabilities satisfied with the services they are receiving? Perhaps even more fundamental is the frequency, or infrequency, of agencies and service providers attempting to solicit feedback from their clients who have MR/DD. The authors note that what little work has been done in this area is probably slanted toward the positive side. Respondents may be self-selected, or have a vested interest, or have a legitimate fear that a poor evaluation may result in a service being eliminated. A state survey conducted in Georgia in the late 1980s is reviewed and a number of implications are pertinent for those providing recreation or leisure programs. Overall satisfaction with a range of services ran from 69 to 100%. One of the weaknesses noted (and this theme runs throughout a number of manuscripts in this monograph) was a lack of trained professionals. Many were not receiving services they desired such as employment and transportation. Regarding recreation and leisure, those adults with MR/DD who were included in the sample expressed a satisfaction with life in general (75%) and one of the factors responsible for this was leisure involvement and relationships with others. While 70% were satisfied with how time was spent, more social programs and after school or work and weekend activities were desired. Eighty-seven percent indicated they were happy with recreation and leisure opportunities, although not enough services or inappropriate services were noted as problems. These relatively high ratings should be considered with the previously mentioned tendencies in mind. The authors close with provocative thoughts on research and evaluation as related to this population. Qualitative methods may be particularly appropriate–the use of interviews, observations, focus groups, and multiple data collection sources is addressed. While the current older group with MR/DD may have had limited opportunities during their lives to make choices or become empowered, they should, nevertheless, be approached frequently to assess success of services provided. It would seem that researchers interested in leisure and retirement for this group should gather at symposia or conferences in order to establish a future research agenda. More empirical studies are being conducted and published in the literature and priorities need to be agreed upon so that theory may continue to be refined and model interventions tested so that practitioners and clients may benefit.

Hoge and Wilhite, as the title "Integration and Leisure Education for Older Adults with Developmental Disabilities" suggests, cover methods and processes of moving selected adults with MR/DD into community programs and experiences. As a necessary element of that transition, leisure education will assist consumers and staff in understanding attitudes, desires, and values held by those considering greater participation in community offerings. An eight-step model is presented beginning with defining who is best suited for integration, and moving to determining needs and preparing staff and clients, and concluding with consumers who feel empowered along with an evaluation of the entire process. The authors primarily focus upon leisure education strategies developed by Joswiak, Beck-Ford and Brown, and the Wake Leisure Education Model developed through the Center for Recreation and Disabilities Studies at the University of North Carolina. None were specifically developed for older adults with MR/DD although Hoge and Wilhite note that adaptations should result in success. This review including others beyond the three noted above provides assistance to staff looking for ways to begin leisure education activities. Many of these leisure education activities could become a part of the total programming offered at group homes or other sites. As the education process progressed, one would expect clients and staff to benefit through a clearer understanding of what is desired, what options are available, and what skills or abilities need to be developed or strengthened. As in other areas noted previously, leisure education models and materials need to be field-tested specifically with aging adults having developmental disabilities. A reporting of strengths and successes would be quite useful for practitioners looking for direction.

Tedrick, in reviewing themes and issues surfacing in the previous chapters, focuses upon the notion of retirement applied to this population and training concerns of those who work with aging adults having developmental disabilities. Many questions raised by authors suggest a research agenda. While on the positive side more is being written and reported, there still exists a need for continued efforts at expanding knowledge so that services and quality of life may improve for mature adults with mental retardation or other developmental disabilities.

Ted Tedrick, PhD

REFERENCE

Keller, M. J. (1991). Activities with developmentally disabled elderly and older adults. New York: The Haworth Press, Inc.

Chapter 1

Older Adults
with Developmental Disabilities:
A Brief Examination of Current Knowledge

Rosangela Boyd

In January of 1995, a White House Conference on Aging and Developmental Disabilities was held in New York. The fact that this is the first White House Conference to address this topic, points to the increased attention being paid to this population. In the past two decades, the amount of information accumulated regarding this topic grew significantly as a result of the heightened visibility of this group in the United States. Among the factors contributing to this greater visibility are: (a) the advances in medical technology leading to extended life expectancy, (b) the deinstitutionalization movement opening doors for community participation, and (c) the shift from a focus primarily on children with developmental disabilities to encompass the entire lifespan.

The earlier studies on aging and developmental disabilities centered around the issues of defining the population, in terms of demographic and functional and characteristics (Baroff, 1982; Blake, 1981; Cotten, Sison and Starr, 1981; Di Giovanni, 1978;

Rosangela Boyd, PhD, CTRS, is Associate Professor, Department of Sport Management and Leisure Studies, Temple University.

[Haworth co-indexing entry note]: "Older Adults with Developmental Disabilities: A Brief Examination of Current Knowledge." Boyd, Rosangela. Co-published simultaneously in *Activities, Adaptation & Aging* (The Haworth Press, Inc.) Vol. 21, No. 3, 1997, pp. 7-27; and: *Older Adults with Developmental Disabilities and Leisure: Issues, Policy, and Practice* (ed: Ted Tedrick) The Haworth Press, Inc., 1997, pp. 7-27. Single or multiple copies of this article are available for a fee from The Haworth Document Delivery Service [1-800-342-9678, 9:00 a.m. - 5:00 p.m. (EST). E-mail address: getinfo@haworth.com].

Janicki and Jacobson, 1982). A second thrust of investigation observed in the literature relates to service provision and needs (Anderson, Lakin, Bruininks, and Hill, 1987; Benz, Halpern and Close, 1986; Krauss and Seltzer, 1986; Seltzer, 1988). A logical follow up was the concentration on issues of planning and public policy leading to demonstration projects (Janicki and Keefe, 1992; LePore and Janicki, 1990; Overynder and Powers, 1987; Seltzer, 1988; Stroud and Sutton, 1988). It was during the late 80s that more emphasis on leisure related concerns started to be discussed more consistently in the literature. Studies focused on levels of leisure participation and projects introducing leisure interventions, as well as structured efforts towards retirement planning and community integration (Anderson et al., 1988; Cotten, 1991; Edelson, 1990; Halan, 1990; Hawkins, 1991; Janicki and Keefe, 1992; Stroud and Sutton, 1988). Although efforts to elucidate some of the points raised in past studies are still apparent, more specific investigation has been initiated in areas such as Down syndrome and Cerebral Palsy, recognizing the diversity of the population of older persons with developmental disabilities (Buchanan, 1990; Harper and Wadsworth, 1990; Hawkins, Eklund, and Martz, 1992; Hestnes, Sand and Fostland, 1991; Overynder, Turk, Dalton, and Janicki, 1992).

The research conducted in this area, although not offering definitive answers to some questions, has helped advance the knowledge of issues related to the provision of leisure services to persons with developmental disabilities undergoing the aging process. The following sections will provide updates on the areas of demographic characteristics, functional skills, and programmatic options in leisure.

DEMOGRAPHIC CHARACTERISTICS

In spite of the many epidemiological studies concluded in the past, national statistics still lack accuracy. Estimates vary from 200,000 (Baroff, 1982) to over 1,300,000 older adults with developmental disabilities in the U.S. (Seltzer and Seltzer, 1985). Some of the problems involved in developing precise figures include the large number of individuals still unknown to formal service providers, the variety of prevalence rates being used and the lack of agreement regarding how this population should be defined.

According to Seltzer (1989), only 40% of the population of older persons with mental retardation, for example, is known to the service network. Prevalence rates used range from 1% to 3% of the general population. Defining what constitutes aging among persons with developmental disabilities has not been an easy task for researchers and policy makers. A review of literature indicates that age marks vary from age 50 (Baker, Seltzer and Seltzer, 1977 to age 65 (Jacobson, Sutton and Janick, 1985). Since the reauthorization of the Older Americans Act in 1987, extending provisions to older persons with disabilities, many states have started to utilize age 60 as a basis for planning (Janicki, 1994). The problem often encountered with this cutoff age is that there is evidence of earlier onset of aging for some members of the population of persons with developmental disabilities, who may remain outside the service network unless an earlier age mark is used. Seltzer and Krauss (1987) recommend age 55 for the purpose of definition and eligibility for services.

In spite of the disagreement surrounding the definition of aging and developmental disabilities, experts in this area concur that the numbers are growing steadily. By the year 2000, the population of persons with developmental disabilities over age 55 is expected to increase by 39%; and by the year 2020, it is supposed to grow by 87% in comparison to 1985 (Jacobson, Sutton, and Janicki, 1985). This steadfast increase has implications for leisure service providers, especially when the current trends toward community inclusion are considered. Not only will there be more persons with developmental disabilities in the community, but also there will be more emphasis on meaningful post-retirement programs to cater to those who are aging and may no longer be appropriate candidates for vocational or day rehabilitation services.

FUNCTIONAL SKILLS

Studies conducted with the purpose of comparing aging persons with and without developmental disabilities indicate that the aging process follows a similar path for both groups (DiGiovanni, 1978; Cotten et al., 1981; Waltz, Harper and Wilson, 1986; Adlin, 1993). Referring to the more recent longitudinal studies which have found changes to occur much later than previously assumed, Adlin (1993) writes, "Many conditions that have been attributed to normal aging, may in fact result from specific diseases, environmental factors, or deconditioning due to disuse" (p. 49). For some persons with developmental disabilities age-related changes may seem greater because of the interaction with already existing deficits resulting from the particular disability; therefore, the line between aging changes and lifelong disability is sometimes blurred.

Physical Domain

As noted by Hawkins and Kultgen (1990), there is considerable agreement regarding the onset of motoric and sensory declines in the fifties and the maintenance or improvement of other skills, such as intellectual function and activities of daily living, through the seventies. It is also common knowledge that certain groups experience pre-mature aging. According to Lucchino (1995), three conditions can be used as predictors of pre-mature aging: (a) lifelong mental retardation associated with Down syndrome and cerebral palsy, (b) early onset of lifelong disabilities such as polio or cerebral palsy, and (c) lifestyle induced disabilities caused by factors such as poor nutrition, alcoholism and high stress. Yet another circumstance associated with earlier decline and consequent reduction in life-expectancy is prolonged institutionalization (Jacobson et al., 1985).

The current focus on disability specific studies may help elucidate the risk factors associated with certain disabilities such as polio, cerebral palsy, and Down syndrome. For persons affected by polio, there is evidence that the virus may be reactivated as persons age, causing further disability (Shapiro, 1994). Although few studies are available, Adlin (1993) offers some possible consequences of the aging process to persons with this motor disorder, based on the secondary complications often associated it. Some of these consequences are: (a) increase in mobility problems, possibly related to degenerative joint disease, (b) greater risk for osteoporosis due to impaired mobility and low levels of calcium and vitamin D, (c) increased difficulties with ventilation and speech, and (d) higher rates of sensory impairment.

Individuals with Down syndrome have experienced a dramatic increase in life expectancy in the last 50 years due to advances in medical technology. It has risen from 9 years (Penrose, 1949) to 55 years (Eyman, Call and White, 1989), with some living to their 70s and 80s (Machemer, 1993). Hearing loss may be a problem pre-existing the aging process, which may become more serious as persons with Down syndrome age. Conductive and sensorineural hearing loss may be developed as early as in childhood and young adulthood respectively (Adlin, 1993). Another sensory deficit which may be experienced is cataracts, which affects approximately 50% of adults with Down syndrome (Hestnes et al., 1991). There is also evidence that persons with Down syndrome undergo premature aging of the immune system (Levin, Nir and Molgimer, 1975; Rabinowe, Rubin, George, and Eisenbarth, 1989). Cardiovascular problems may also be intensified for these individuals due to the high incidence–40%–of congenital heart disease (Adlin, 1993). Musculoskeletal problems identified for this population which, combined with age changes, may pose challenges for independent functioning include decreased muscle tone, scoliosis, ligamentous laxity and a high incidence of bunions–90%–all of which may affect mobility (Diamond, Lynne, and Sigman, 1981, Adlin, 1993).

Another aspect which has been well established is that persons with Down syndrome often develop Alzheimer's disease at an earlier age than the general population. The average onset of the disease is 53-55 years (Adlin, 1993), and the average duration ranges from 3.5 to 10.5 years (Dalton and Wisniewski, 1990). In the past, it was believed that the incidence of Alzheimer's disease was higher for persons with Down syndrome and that all persons who lived long enough would develop it. This assumption was partially based on the finding that the neuropathological changes associated with the disease occur in 100% of persons with Down syndrome. In spite of the presence of such changes in the brain, however, only 40-45% of those between 50 and 70 years old will develop the disease. This percentage is not radically different from that of the general older population–50%–when age 85 is used as the identifying variable (Machemer, 1993). It is true that at age 50, there is a higher incidence of Alzheimer's disease in persons with Down syndrome than in the general population, but this may reflect the earlier onset of aging rather than a greater predisposition to develop the disease.

From the issues mentioned above, some implications for leisure service providers seem clear. With a number of the physical conditions outlined, exercise appears to be a desirable intervention. A number of benefits have been attributed to exercise. In summarizing them, Dangott and Kalish (1979) describe exercise as "the closest thing to an anti-aging and anti-disease pill" (p. 68). While exercises such as weight lifting and calisthenics may improve muscle flexibility and strength and prevent osteoporosis, others such as swimming, walking and cycling may enhance cardiovascular functions. Water exercises have also been recommended for persons who need to work on range of motion. Aside from the physical benefits, exercise has the potential to positively impact psychological well being, socialization and cognitive functioning (Leitner and Leitner, 1985; Teaff, 1985).

The development of educational programs connected to leisure delivery agencies is also warranted. Some of the conditions described in the previous paragraphs may be worsened or ameliorated by changes in lifestyle such as diet, physical activity and medical checkups. Currently, there is little information available in accessible language and alternate formats regarding the aging process to empower individuals and their families. Both individuals with disabilities and their caregivers would benefit from receiving information on how to control health conditions by eliminating some risk factors and preventing secondary complications resulting from developmental disabilities.

Psychosocial Domain

Longitudinal studies conducted by Edgerton and associates (Seltzer, 1993) have shown an increase in life satisfaction during the 30 years that followed deinstitutionalization for individuals with mild mental retardation. A study conducted by Hawkins (1993) revealed that age had a significantly negative impact on life satisfaction. The older the person with developmental disabilities was, the lower the life satisfaction. Age was also a detrimental factor for persons with Down syndrome when leisure activity was considered, with the number of leisure activities declining with age. The study also uncovered a factor of relevance for leisure professionals. For persons without Down syndrome, a positive correlation between leisure participation and life satisfaction was shown while a negative correlation was found for desire to increase leisure participation. It appears that individuals who wanted to expand their leisure participation experienced a lower life satisfaction, which might result from the lack of opportunities to satisfy their desire for more participation. These findings point to the importance of providing a variety of leisure activities to persons with developmental disabilities.

In the area of social support and social inclusion, there is reason to believe that persons with developmental disabilities are at a disadvantage. When patterns of social involvement are compared, it becomes apparent that differences exist. Older adults with developmental disabilities are less likely to have experienced marriage, procreation and the common sources of social interaction available to the average citizen, such as community job placement, community residence and inclusion in civic and recreational activities. Their sources of social support come primarily from family members, staff and other persons with disabilities. For those still residing at home, family members play the most important role in providing support, while for those living in institutional or community settings, friends were the major providers of emotional support and companionship (Krauss and Erickson, 1988). A logical consequence of these dynamics is the crises experienced when relocation is needed. A study by Seltzer, Finally and Howell, 1988 showed nursing home residents to have less contact with family and community members than those in community residences (Seltzer, Finally and Howell, 1988). Anderson (1993) compared residents of group homes, foster homes, large private facilities and state institutions regarding household integration, leisure/recreation integration, social relationships and community resource use. Findings included (a) a negative correlation between age and household and community inclusion, (b) residents of group homes had higher levels of household and community integration but lower levels of social relationships than residents of foster homes, (c) residents of large private facilities and state institutions had lower levels of social relationships than foster homes, (d) residents of state institutions scored lower on inclusion than residents of foster homes. Additional data analysis indicated that a large number of residents in all settings reported having no friends outside the staff or family. The lack of interaction with persons in the community is an alarming finding which seems suitable for change by the efforts to include older adults with developmental disabilities in the community in programs frequented by other older adults such as senior centers and adult day care. Leisure professionals should not forget, though, that intergenerational contacts are also needed and that community integration may go beyond the boundaries of the aging system.

PROGRAMMATIC ISSUES IN LEISURE

Studies in the area of leisure involvement have uncovered a limited pattern of participation among older persons with developmental disabilities, particularly for those residing in institutions. The types of activities engaged in frequently tend to be of a passive type. When community outings are discussed, they are usually described as group trips led by staff, during which there are few opportunities for individuals to interact with the general population.

A Profile of Leisure Patterns

A study by Benz, Halper and Close (1986) found that the participation of nursing home residents in outside day programs was significantly lower than residents of community or public residential facilities. It also showed a large number of individuals who did not participate in any activities, either inside or outside the home. The only activities engaged in by over half of the residents were watching television and listening to the radio. Activities such as going to a library or attending a senior center program were mentioned by less than 10% of the participants. The residents who were more likely to participate in leisure activities were typically male, younger and more mobile. When the staff was asked to justify the low participation levels, 61% indicated residents' lack of abilities as impeding. However, the study clearly showed that no differences existed in skill level between males and females and that the older residents were indeed less disabled than the younger ones. The fact that one third of the residents used wheelchairs may have led to the perceptions of lack of ability. The findings point to a lack of expertise on the part of staff in distinguishing between level of disability and capacity to benefit from community programs.

The tendency to participate in activities of a passive nature was documented by other studies as well. Using data from a national study, Anderson and his associates (1987) noted that activities such as watching television, listening to the radio and playing records were popular among 90% of the residents, regardless of what type of facility they resided in. The study confirmed the low level of participation in leisure activities by individuals residing in institutions. Watching television and listening to the radio were also among the most common activities engaged by the members of project ACCESS in Ohio, as reported by Stroud and Sutton (1988). A more recent study conducted by Hawkins (1991) again found these activities to be among the top ten most frequent ones for a group of older persons with mental retardation in Indiana.

Other activities mentioned by participants in the surveys mentioned above include going out to eat, shopping, attending church, going to parties, going for rides and visiting with friends. The concerning aspect of this list is that they either represent activities pursued with other residents in the residential site or outings where residents stay together as a group, often calling attention to their disability and seldom interacting with other members of the community. Such patterns violate Wofensberger's (1983) social role valorization principle and efforts towards full community inclusion.

The fact that participation may be limited does not necessarily reflect the interests of persons with developmental disabilities. Studies have also shown that when asked if they wished to expand their leisure involvement by either increasing participation in activities already pursued or engaging in new activities, respondents mentioned a variety of activities that ranged from socialization activities such as traveling to be with friends and families, going out to dinner and movies, having picnics, going to concerts and going to parties, to hobbies such as taking photographs and playing an instrument. Also common were sport related activities such as: swimming, fishing, golfing, playing baseball and volleyball, bicycling and running (Anderson et al., 1987; Hawkins 1991). An interesting factor, deserving further attention by investigators, was the lack of interest among persons with Down syndrome to engage in new activities or increase the frequency of participation in current activities (Hawkins, 1993).

It is true that most of the activities mentioned by the surveys reflect core activities also typical of the older lifespan stages. The problem, though, lies with several issues. First, these activities were not simply activities that older persons with developmental disabilities chose to remain engaged in after years of exploring different types of pursuits. Surveys with younger adults show similar trends in leisure involvement. Secondly, due to the challenges faced by individuals with a life history of low physical activity and social segregation, it is especially important to offer them opportunities to choose activities which will help them overcome some of these challenges. Thirdly, as the survey also indicated, they do wish to seek new activities. And, lastly, it may be a mistake to believe that limited participation reflects individual choice. Some of the individuals being served by leisure professionals today have a history of institutionalization, thus being accustomed to having others structure their lives. Their ability to make informed decisions is low and their awareness of the options available to them is limited. Research also provides evidence of some of these limitations. When the question about barriers limiting participation was raised the most common answers mentioned included conditions beyond the individuals' immediate control such as transportation, lack of equipment, shortage of companions, and unavailability of certain activities and facilities (Anderson et al., 1987; Hawkins 1991). Nevertheless, there were other barriers such as lack of knowledge and problems with decision making, which may be corrected by the implementation of programs such as leisure education. Training in the areas of leisure awareness, resources and skills may eliminate some of the individual barriers, thus empowering consumers to expand their leisure behavior.

Retirement Issues

Retirement has become a social institution marking a new stage in the lifespan of average Americans. If the concept of normalization is to be applied for persons with developmental disabilities, retirement should also be an option to them. Among professionals working with this population, there are mixed feelings regarding the implementation of retirement programs. Some feel that work is too valuable for persons with disabilities and should not be taken away from them. Others claim that the creation of structured retirement (Blaney, 1991; Sutton, Sterns and Park, 1993) programs present an alternative to vocational programs and are realistic and necessary, particularly considering the importance of finding ways to deal with time and the need to offer individuals a wide range of options for later life.

A variety of differences are evident when persons with developmental disabilities are compared with other American citizens. Their work history may be different; sheltered workshop and some supported employment represent the most common types of work related activities among this group. Without a long history of full time employment, retirement benefits, which usually become an incentive for most workers, are not a possibility for this group. The value placed upon work also seems greater for persons with developmental disabilities. They realize that work is valued in American society, their friendships and social interactions are centered in the workplace, and, perhaps, most important, it is the source of discretionary funds (Sutton et al., 1993, p. 99). Work is a source of self-worth and also a way to structure time. Studies have shown that people with developmental disabilities prefer structured time activities to leisure time (Stroud, Roberts and Murphy, 1986). The reluctance to have free time may derive from the lack of decision making skills previously discussed.

The need for pre-retirement programs is a logical consequence. If the benefits of retirement are not explored and if the individual is not aware of the existence of meaningful avocational activities. From interviews conducted with participants of a pre-retirement program, Cotten and Laughlin (1989) reported an initial negative attitude towards retirement due to a perceived lack of alternatives. Attitudes did improve, however, after exposure to the advantages of retirement and options available to them. Yet, a study conducted in Ohio reported that 47% of the sites surveyed offered no preparation for the lifestyle change associated with retirement (Sutton et al., 1993). A few specific programs have been developed to assist persons with developmental disabilities prepare for retirement (Cheseldine, 1992; Jackson, 1992). As more agencies implement such programs, persons with developmental disabilities are expected to experience an easier transition into retirement.

The perspective of retirement as just the continuation of individual growth through alternative activities is expressed in Cotten's definition: "retirement is graduation to another stage in the development of the individual. It is not and cannot be synonymous with the term quitting. Going home, regardless of how lovely the home is and rocking is not retirement. That is quitting" (1994, p. 90). The author points to the need to explore new interests and friendships, and to engage in activities of the person's own informed choosing as part of a successful retirement program. He also warns against treating individuals with developmental disabilities as groups or masses, thus forgetting the heterogeneous nature of this population. The diversity within this population calls for a variety of creative alternatives to retirement. Options may range from participation in senior citizens or adult day care programs with other older adults to inter-generational community integrated activities, to specialized programs within the developmental system.

Community Integration

In 1987, two actions of congress recognized the need for collaboration between the aging system and developmental disabilities system. Amendments to both the Older Americans Act and the Developmental Disabilities Act were made to encourage the two systems to work jointly to better serve older persons with developmental disabilities (Janicki, 1988).

The projects created as a result have included a variety of approaches. One of the most common approaches is the integration of older persons with disabilities into senior centers. All over the country, integration efforts are being reported (Baltes, 1992; Dittman, 1992; Rancourt, 1989; Rylander, 1992; Vadnais, 1992; Wade, 1992; Wickeman and Gould, 1992; Zimpel, 1991). Other projects include the inclusion of persons with developmental disabilities into adult day care centers, particularly those utilizing the social model (Hughes and Hammond, 1992; Searles, 1992; Sears, 1992). The use of senior companions was mentioned by a variety of programs as an asset to the integration of persons with disabilities into the agencies serving the older population (Carter, 1992; Goodman, 1992; Rancourt, 1989; Stroud and Sutton, 1988; Turner and Bryant, 1992). Senior companions act as bridges for community integration, facilitating the entrance of persons with disabilities into community agencies and helping them interact with other participants. Positive outcomes such as improvement in interpersonal skills and self-esteem have been reported in association with community integration programs (LePore and Janicki, 1990; Stroud and Sutton, 1988).

Other types of programs show creative approaches to integrating persons with developmental disabilities into community activities, taking into consideration their preferences and skills. Two of such projects include the "Syncopated Seniors" and the "Community Garden Project" (Janicki and Keefe, 1992). The first project involved the organization of a chorus group bringing together seniors with and without developmental disabilities. The second project centered around the integration of seniors with developmental disabilities into a community gardening project. In both projects, adults with developmental disabilities were able to interact with community members and to be seen in a positive light by them in a true example of social role valorization. The projects also exemplify the possibility of encountering community options that cater to the specific interests of persons with developmental disabilities as individuals.

In all the projects discussed above, a number of factors contributed to the eventual success reported: (a) participants were carefully chosen, (b) social skills training of participants preceded integration efforts, (c) training of companions and staff was conducted prior to implementation, (d) gradual steps were taken to foster integration and decrease the likelihood for rejection, and (e) a sharing of experiences was encouraged, with benefits of participation being presented to everyone involved.

Options Within the System

Although community integration is desirable to all persons with disabilities, professionals should not expect to effect changes without careful preparation. Some older adults with developmental disabilities may not possess the social skills needed for full inclusion into community programs. Their forced entry into community agencies may have disastrous results and close doors to future participants. Therefore, there is a need for programs within the developmental disabilities system which will provide alternatives to work and prepare seniors for future placement in more integrated settings. Some examples of senior centers and other programs built within agencies serving persons with developmental disabilities have been successful (Smith and Lafontaine, 1992; Stone, 1992; Streaks, 1992). Such initiatives may be particularly needed in creating positive experiences for seniors in rural areas where there is a limited number of senior services available and penetration into the aging system may be difficult at first.

In defining the characteristics of ideal day services, Kutgen (1989) pointed to the following: (a) replacement of functions of work, (b) accessible physical environment and social climate, (c) leisure as a developmental task, (d) reality orientation, (e) health maintenance and prevention, (f) social friendships and prevention, (g) understanding the aging process, and (h) life review and grief counseling.

A variety of innovative programs involving leisure have been developed, including the areas of physical fitness through activities such as rowing (Engerman and Pederson, 1989), and arts and crafts (Edelson, 1991; Harlan, 1991; Clements, 1992). Benefits of participation in the fitness program included improvement in muscle strength and cardiovascular measures. Participants in the arts and crafts programs had psychosocial gains in areas such as socialization skills, ability to express preferences, capacity to select materials and initiate work independently, and self-image enhancement. Activities such as these may prepare older adults with disabilities to join similar community programs. They may also fulfill the need to remain engaged in productive activities. In the case of Edelson's art and crafts program, for example, participants were trained in art modalities and encouraged to produce and sell items of professional quality, according to their skill level.

SUMMARY

As the number of older adults with developmental disabilities living in the community increases, leisure professionals will be called to replace vocational services with stimulating activities in a variety of settings, including home and community agencies serving both senior citizens and individuals of all ages. This article outlined a number of reasons why leisure services are of great importance for this population. Leisure provides opportunities for socialization, productivity and feelings of self-worth often encountered at work; therefore, it has a meaningful role in retirement. Leisure activities may also improve fitness levels and maintain physical skills which tend to decline earlier for persons with developmental disabilities than other older adults. In the psychosocial area, there is evidence that life satisfaction is correlated with leisure involvement. Leisure settings are also conducive to inclusion. Given the history of segregation shared by many older adults with developmental disabilities, it is important to promote community integration within the aging system and beyond. With the paradigm shift toward empowering the individual to make choices and actively engage in person centered planning, leisure professionals are left with the crucial role of helping older adults with disabilities in making informed choices regarding their leisure lifestyle. Leisure education is a necessary intervention, which must be adapted to the cognitive levels and age-related changes observed in this group of older adults. In summary, the issue of quality of life for older persons with developmental disabilities, be it in the physical or psychosocial domains, is closely related to the functions leisure can play in their lives. By implementing programs that meet major goals while taking into account the ability of the individuals involved for self-determination, leisure professionals may have a positive impact in the lives of older adults with life long disabilities.

AUTHOR NOTE

The author served on the Board of Directors of the American Therapeutic Recreation Association from 1994 to 1996. Her research interests include the efficacy of recreation interventions in long-term care, minority aging, and older adults with developmental disabilities. She has recently co-authored the book, *Leisure and Aging: Ulyssean Living in Later Life* (Sagamore Publishing) with Fran McGuire and Ted Tedrick.

REFERENCES

Anderson, D. (1993). Social inclusion of older adults with mental retardation. In E. Sutton, A. Factor, B. Hawkins, T. Heller, and G. Seltzer, *Older adults with developmental disabilities: Optimizing choice and change.* Baltimore, MD: Paul H. Brookes.

Anderson, D., Lakin, K., Bruininks, R. and Hill, B. (1987) *A national study of residential and support services for elderly persons with mental retardation.* Minneapolis: University of Minnesota, Department of Educational Psychology.

Adlin, M. (1993). Health care issues. In E. Sutton, A. Factor, B. Hawkins, T. Heller, and G. Seltzer, *Older adults with developmental disabilities: Optimizing choice and change.* Baltimore, MD: Paul H. Brookes.

Baker, B., Seltzer, G., and Seltzer, M. (1985). *As close as possible: Community residences for retarded adults.* Boston, MA: Little, Brown and Co.

Balch, M. (1992). Silver streaks. In M. Janicki and R. Keefe (eds.) *Integration experiences casebook: Program ideas in aging and developmental disabilities.* New York, NY: New York State Office of Mental Retardation and Developmental Disabilities.

Baltes, P. (1992). WACOSA Seniors. In M. Janicki and R. Keefe (eds.) *Integration experiences casebook: Program ideas in aging and developmental disabilities.* New York, NY: New York State Office of Mental Retardation and Developmental Disabilities.

Baroff, G. (1982). Predicting the prevalence of mental retardation in individual catchment areas. *Mental Retardation, 20,* 133-135.

Benz, M., Halpern, A. and Close, D. (1986). Access to day programs and leisure activities by nursing home residents with mental retardation. *Mental Retardation, 24* (3), 147-152.

Blake, R. (1981). Disabled older persons: A demographic analysis. *Journal of Rehabilitation, 47* (4), 19-27.

Blaney, B. (1990). *Planning a vision: A resource handbook on aging and developmental disabilities.* Cambridge, MA: Human Services Research Institute.

Buchanan, L. (1990). Early onset of presbicusis in Down syndrome. *Scandinavian Audiology, 19,* 103-110.

Carter, E. (1992). Senior integration project. In M. Janicki and R. Keefe (eds.), *Integration experiences casebook: Program ideas in aging and developmental disabilities.* New York, NY: New York State Office of Mental Retardation and Developmental Disabilities.

Cheseldine, S. (1992). Step forward retirement coaching. In M. Janicki and R. Keefe (eds.), *Integration experiences casebook: Program ideas in aging and developmental disabilities.* New York, NY: New York State Office of Mental Retardation and Developmental Disabilities.

Clements, C. (1992). *The arts and fitness quality of life program.* Athens, GA: University of Georgia.

Cotten, P. (1991). Retirement planning workbook. *American Association on Mental Retardation, Aging/MR Interest Group Newsletter, 15* (1/2), 13.

Cotten, P. (1994). *Retirement "to" something.* National Conference on aging and Disabilities: A vision for the future, Conference proceedings, North Dakota, Center for Developmental Disabilities.

Cotten, P., Sison, G. and Starr, S. (1981). Comparing elderly mentally retarded and non-mentally retarded individuals: Who are they? What are their needs? *The Gerontologist, 21:359-365.*

Cotten, P. and Laughlin, C. (1989). Retirement: a new career. *American Association on Mental Retardation, Aging/MR Interest Group Newsletter, 15* (1/2), 13.

Dangott, L. and Kalish, R. (1979). *A time to enjoy: The pleasures of aging.* Englewood Cliffs, NJ: Prentice-Hall.

Diamond, L., Lynne, D. and Sigman, B. (1981). Orthopedic Disorders in Patients with Down Syndrome. *Orthopedic Clinics in North America, 15,* 57-71.

DiGiovanni, L. (1978). The elderly retarded: A little known group. *The Gerontologist, 18* (3), 262-266.

Dittman, L. (1992). SARAH's elder enrichment program. In M. Janicki and R. Keefe (eds.), *Integration experiences casebook: Program ideas in aging and developmental disabilities.* New York, NY: New York State Office of Mental Retardation and Developmental Disabilities.

Dubiel-Turgeon, B. (1992). Community garden project. In M. Janicki and R. Keefe (eds.), *Integration experiences casebook: Program ideas in aging and developmental disabilities.* New York, NY: New York State Office of Mental Retardation and Developmental Disabilities.

Edelson, R. (1990). Arts and Crafts, not "arts and crafts"–Alternative vocational day activities for adults who are older and mentally retarded. *Activities, Adaptation & Aging, 15,* (1/2), 81-98.

Engeman, M. and Pederson, E. (1989). *Interdisciplinary health promotion program on aging adults with mental retardation.* Cincinnati, OH: University Affiliated Center for Developmental Disabilities. *Activities, Adaptation & Aging, 15,* (1/2), 67-80.

Eyman, R., Call, T. and White, J. (1989). Mortality of elderly mentally retarded persons in California. *Journal of Applied Gerontology, 8,* 203-215.

Goodman, R. (1992). JASA outreach project. In M. Janicki and R. Keefe (eds.), *Integration experiences casebook: Program ideas in aging and developmental disabilities.* New York, NY: New York State Office of Mental Retardation and Developmental Disabilities.

Harlan, J. (1990). The use of art therapy for older adults with developmental disabilities. *Activities, Adaptation & Aging, 15*(1/2), 67-80.

Harper, D. and Wadsworth, J. (1990). Dementia and depression in elders with mental retardation: A pilot study. *Research in Developmental Disabilities, 11,* 177-198.

Hawkins, B. (1991) An exploration of adaptive skills and leisure activity of older adults with mental retardation. *Therapeutic Recreation Journal, 25*(4), 9-28.

Hawkins, B. (1993). Leisure participation and life satisfaction of older adults with mental retardation and Down syndrome. In E. Sutton, A. Factor, B. Hawkins, T. Heller, and G. Seltzer, *Older adults with developmental disabilities: Optimizing choice and change.* Baltimore, MD: Paul H. Brookes.

Hawkins, B. and Kultgen, P. (1990). Activities and adaptation: A call for innovations to serve aging adults with developmental disabilities. *Activities, Adaptation & Aging, 15*(1/2), 5-18.

Hawkins, B., Eklund, S., and Martz, B. (1992). *Detecting aging-related declines in adults with developmental disabilities: A research monograph.* Cincinnati, OH: Rehabilitation Research and training center Consortium on Aging and Developmental Disabilities.

Hestnes, A., Sand, T. and Fostland, K. (1991). Ocular findings in Down's syndrome. *Journal of Mental Deficiency Research, 31,* 31-39.

Hughes, B. and Hammond, J. (1992). Adult dynamics day program. In M. Janicki and R. Keefe (eds.), *Integration experiences casebook: Program ideas in aging and developmental disabilities.* New York, NY: New York State Office of Mental Retardation and Developmental Disabilities.

Jackson, A. (1992). SLARC Retirement coaching. In M. Janicki and R. Keefe (eds.), *Integration experiences casebook: Program ideas in aging and developmental disabilities.* New York, NY: New York State Office of Mental Retardation and Developmental Disabilities.

Jacobson, J., Sutton, M., and Janicki, M. (1985). Demography and characteristics of aging and aged mentally retarded persons. In M. Janicki and H. Wisniewski (eds.), *Aging and developmental disabilities: Issues and approaches.* Baltimore, MD: Paul H. Brookes.

Janicki, M. (1988). Symposium overview: Aging, the challenge. *Mental retardation, 26*(4), 177-180.

Janicki, M. (1994). *A vision for the future: Aging and developmental disabilities working together.* National Conference on Aging and Disabilities: A vision for the future, Conference proceedings, North Dakota, Center for Developmental Disabilities.

Janicki, M. and Jacobson, J. (1982). The character of developmental disabilities in New York state: Preliminary observations. *Journal of Rehabilitation Research, 5* (2), 191-202.

Janicki, M. and Keefe, R. (1992). *Integration experiences casebook: Program ideas in aging and developmental disabilities.* New York, NY: New York State Office of Mental Retardation and Developmental Disabilities.

Krauss, M. and Erikson, M. (1988). Informal support networks among aging persons with mental retardation. *Mental Retardation, 26*(4), 197-202.

Krauss, M. and Seltzer, M. (1986). Comparison of elderly and adult retarded persons in community and institutional settings. *American Journal of Mental Deficiency, 91,* 237-243.

Krauss, M. and Seltzer, M. (1988). *Planning for the future: Meeting the needs of elderly developmentally disabled persons* (vol #1), Waltham, MA: Brandeis University, studies on Aging and Developmental Disabilities.

Kultgen, P. (1990). Day services In B. Hawkins, S. Eklund and R. Gaetani (eds.), *Aging and Developmental Disabilities: A training inservice package.* Bloomington, IN: Indiana University, Institute for the Study of Developmental Disabilities.

Laughlin, C., Cotten, P. and Simpson, J. (1992). Mississippi retirement skills teaching program. In M. Janicki and R. Keefe (eds) *Integration experiences casebook: Program ideas in aging and developmental disabilities.* New York, NY: New York State Office of Mental Retardation and Developmental Disabilities.

Leitner, M. and Leitner, S. (1985) *Leisure in later life: A sourcebook for the provision of recreational services for elders.* New York, NY: The Haworth Press, Inc.

LePore, P. and Janicki, M. (1990). *The wit to win: How to integrate older persons with developmental disabilities into community aging programs.* Albany, NY: New York State Office for Aging.

Levin, S., Nir, E. and Molgimer, B. (1975). T-system immune deficiency in Down's syndrome. *Pediatrics, 56,* 123-126.

Lucchino, R. (1995). *Policy change in the OAA to accommodate those under 60 years of age who are experiencing late onset disabilities due to pre-mature aging.* White House Conference on Aging and developmental Disabilities: New Directions, Policy and Research. New York, Young Adult Institute.

Machemer, R. (1993). Alzheimer's disease and Down syndrome: The connection. In R. Machemer and J. Overynder (eds.), *Understanding aging and developmental disabilities: An in-service curriculum.* Rochester, NY: University of Rochester, Training Program in Aging and Developmental Disabilities.

Overynder, J. and Powers, J. (1987). *Long range planning for community based services to elderly persons with developmental disabilities and their families in Monroe County, New York: A task force report.* Rochester, NY: Rochester University.

Overynder, J., Turk, M., Dalton, A. and Janicki, M. (1992). *I'm worried about the future: The aging of adults with cerebral palsy.* Albany, NY: New York State Developmental Disabilities Council.

Penrose, L. (1949). The incidence of mongolism in the general population. *Journal of Mental Science, 9,* 10.

Rancourt, A. (1989). Older adults with developmental disabilities/mental retardation: Implications for professional services. *Therapeutic Recreation Journal, 23*(1), 47-57.

Rabinowe, S., Rubin, I., George, K., Adri, M. and Eisenbarth, G. (1989). Trissomy 21 Down's syndrome): Autoimmunity aging and monoclonal antibody-defined T-cell abnormalities. *Journal of Autoimmunity, 2,* 25-30.

Rylander, J. (1992). Middletown center project. In M. Janicki and R. Keefe (eds.), *Integration experiences casebook: Program ideas in aging and developmental disabilities.* New York, NY: New York State Office of Mental Retardation and Developmental Disabilities.

Searles, J. (1992). Cattaraugus outreach project. In M. Janicki and R. Keefe (eds.), *Integration experiences casebook: Program ideas in aging and developmental disabilities.* New York, NY: New York State Office of Mental Retardation and Developmental Disabilities.

Sears, C. (1992). Madison county integration program. In M. Janicki and R. Keefe (eds.), *Integration experiences casebook: Program ideas in aging and devel-*

opmental disabilities. New York, NY: New York State Office of Mental Retardation and Developmental Disabilities.

Seltzer, M. (1988). Structure and patterns of service utilization by elderly persons with mental retardation. *Mental Retardation, 26*(4), 181-185.

Seltzer, M. (1989). Introduction to aging and lifelong disabilities: Context for decision making. In E. Ansello and T. Rose (eds.), *Aging and lifelong disabilities: partnership for the 21st century, The Wingspread conference report.* Palm Springs, CA: Elder Press.

Seltzer, G. (1993). Psychological adjustment in midlife persons with mental retardation. In E. Sutton, A. Factor, B. Hawkins, T. Heller, and G. Seltzer, *Older adults with developmental disabilities: Optimizing choice and change.* Baltimore, MD: Paul H. Brookes.

Seltzer, G., Finally, E. and Howell, M. (1988). Functional characteristics of elderly persons with mental retardation in community settings and nursing homes. *Mental Retardation, 26*(4), 25-27.

Seltzer, M. and Krauss, M. (1987). *Aging and mental retardation: Expanding the continuum.* Washington, DC: American Association on Mental Retardation.

Seltzer, G. and Seltzer, M. (1985). The elderly mentally retarded: A group in need of services. *The Journal of Gerontological Social Work, 8,* 99-119.

Smith, M. and Lafontaine, R. (1992). First state senior center. In M. Janicki and R. Keefe (eds.), *Integration experiences casebook: Program ideas in aging and developmental disabilities.* New York, NY: New York State Office of Mental Retardation and Developmental Disabilities.

Stone, J. (1992). Kentucky's rural assistance project. In M. Janicki and R. Keefe (eds.), *Integration experiences casebook: Program ideas in aging and developmental disabilities.* New York, NY: New York State Office of Mental Retardation and Developmental Disabilities.

Stroud, M., Roberts, R. and Murphy, M. (1986). Life status of elderly mentally retarded/developmentally disabled persons in northeast Ohio. In J. Berg (ed.), *Science and service in mental retardation.* London, England: Methuen.

Stroud, M. and Sutton, E. (1988). *Expanding options for older adults with developmental disabilities: A practical guide to achieving community access.* Baltimore, MD: Paul H. Brookes.

Sutton, E., Sterns, H. and Park, L. (1993). Realities of retirement and pre-retirement planning. In E. Sutton, A. Factor, B. Hawkins, T. Heller, and G. Seltzer, *Older adults with developmental disabilities: Optimizing choice and change.* Baltimore, MD: Paul H. Brookes.

Teaff, J. (1985). *Leisure services with the elderly.* Prospect Heights, IL: Waveland Press.

Turner, L. and Bryant, T. (1992). Community based support systems program. In M. Janicki and R. Keefe (eds.), *Integration experiences casebook: Program ideas in aging and developmental disabilities.* New York, NY: New York State Office of Mental Retardation and Developmental Disabilities.

Vadnais, S. (1992). Seniors special needs activities program. In M. Janicki and R. Keefe (eds.), *Integration experiences casebook: Program ideas in aging and developmental disabilities.* New York, NY: New York State Office of Mental Retardation and Developmental Disabilities.

Waltz, T., Harper, D. and Wilson, J. (1986). The aging. In T. Steins and H. Sessoms (eds.), *Recreation and special populations.* Boston, MA: Allyn & Bacon.

Wade, P. (1992). Liberty center project. In M. Janicki and R. Keefe (eds.), *Integration experiences casebook: Program ideas in aging and developmental disabilities.* New York, NY: New York State Office of Mental Retardation and Developmental Disabilities.

Wofensberger, W. (1983). Social role valorization: A proposed new term for the principle of normalization. *Mental Retardation, 21,* 234-239.

Wickeman, K. and Gould, M.(1992). MARC's opportunities for older adults In M. Janicki and R. Keefe (eds.), *Integration experiences casebook: Program ideas in aging and developmental disabilities.* New York, NY: New York State Office of Mental Retardation and Developmental Disabilities.

Zimpel, B. (1990). Sharing activities–The Oneida A.R.C. Cornhill Senior Integration Project. *Activities, Adaptation & Aging, 15*(1/2), 131-140.

Zimpel, B. and Heretz, N. (1992). Syncopated seniors. In M. Janicki and R. Keefe (eds.), *Integration experiences casebook: Program ideas in aging and developmental disabilities.* New York, NY: New York State Office of Mental Retardation and Developmental Disabilities.

Chapter 2

Health, Fitness, and Quality of Life for Older Adults with Developmental Disabilities

Barbara A. Hawkins

BACKGROUND

The aging process brings about life changes in all of us–changes that often result in substantial challenges. A significant body of literature on age-related change in the general population provides a sense of what is normative (see Shock et al., 1984). Physiological decline may include progressive loss in muscular and skeletal functions, diminished cardiac output, and generalized loss in other bodily functions, such as pain sensitivity and temperature control (Rudelli, 1985; Siegel, 1976). Overall intellectual functioning, which remains stable until the late 60s, may begin a gradual decline thereafter. Social-emotional changes and needs associated with later life also have gained increasing recognition as important aspects of growing older.

For persons with mental retardation and other development disabilities, a comparatively smaller body of information about the

Barbara A. Hawkins, ReD, is Associate Professor, Department of Recreation and Park Administration, School of Health, Physical Education and Recreation, Indiana University, Room 133, Bloomington, IN 47405.

[Haworth co-indexing entry note]: "Health, Fitness, and Quality of Life for Older Adults with Developmental Disabilities." Hawkins, Barbara A. Co-published simultaneously in *Activities, Adaptation & Aging* (The Haworth Press, Inc.) Vol. 21, No. 3, 1997, pp. 29-35; and: *Older Adults with Developmental Disabilities and Leisure: Issues, Policy, and Practice* (ed: Ted Tedrick) The Haworth Press, Inc., 1997, pp. 29-35. Single or multiple copies of this article are available for a fee from The Haworth Document Delivery Service [1-800-342-9678, 9:00 a.m. - 5:00 p.m. (EST). E-mail address: getinfo@haworth.com].

29

aging process exists while research efforts have continued to mount over the past 10-20 years. In a recent three year study of age-related change for persons with mental retardation, the findings suggested several interesting patterns in persons with mental retardation (Hawkins, Eklund, & Martz, 1992). For individuals whose mental retardation was caused by Down syndrome, shorter life expectancy overall with an earlier onset of age-related decline was confirmed. For persons whose mental retardation was from other causes, the aging process was not found to be accelerated.

Physiological changes that were associated with aging in persons with mental retardation included: weight, percent body fat, blood pressure, grip strength, vital capacity, vibratory threshold, far vision, hearing, and trunk flexibility (Hawkins, Eklund, & Martz, 1992). Losses in all these areas, with the exception of far vision and hearing, can be modified (slowed) by intervention. Losses in far vision and hearing can be compensated for by wearing glasses and hearing aids.

Cross-sectional findings supported a picture of gender differences in patterns of cognitive functioning with age for subjects with Down syndrome (Hawkins, Eklund, & Martz, 1992). There were clear age differences when comparing males and females in their 30s and 40s. Performance by males appeared to peak in the 30s, while females' performance was not seen to peak until the 40s (or, in some cases, the 50s). For individuals whose mental retardation was not from Down syndrome, there was a similar pattern only at older age levels. Males appeared to peak on most subtests of cognitive functioning in their 60s, while females showed higher performance in their 70s on some subtests. Although gender differences were not quite as marked for persons without Down syndrome compared with individuals with Down syndrome, the trend over the three year study was present.

Measures of functional skills (or adaptive behavior) indicated that aging persons with mental retardation who were not severely, profoundly, or multiply impaired maintained their functional independence for activities used in basic daily living: bathing, dressing, going to the toilet, transferring, continence, feeding, and ambulation (Hawkins, Eklund, & Martz, 1992). In areas that extend beyond these basic skills, however, more assistance was needed; for example, traveling around town, use of medications, use of money, work-related skills, speech, and meal preparation. Again, these areas are amendable to intervention for the purpose of promoting the maintenance of skill levels.

Another important area examined was the number of life events that occurred within a year's time that contributed to increased stress (Hawkins, Eklund, & Martz, 1992). It is often thought (and, perhaps, erroneously so) that people with developmental disabilities are sheltered from many of life's stressful events. This study, however, revealed that aging adults with developmental disabilities experience many of the same stresses common to most adults (e.g., going to the hospital or experiencing serious illness, loss of friends or family members). The value of assessing stress producing events is directly related to the implementation of activities that reduce stressful feelings and responses.

The last area studied by Hawkins, Eklund, and Martz (1992) was social life including leisure patterns, the perception of constraining barriers to leisure participation, and the evaluation of life satisfaction. In this three year study, life satisfaction was significantly related with participation in leisure activities and influenced by the age of the individual. In many of the areas assessed in this mixed cross-sectional and longitudinal study of aging-related change in adults with mental retardation, advancing age was found to be a significant factor (Hawkins, Eklund, & Martz, 1992).

Regarding other types of disabilities common to the broad category of developmental disabilities, however, only limited research data are available. Some recent information has been reported for persons with cerebral palsy (Brown, Bontempo, & Turk, 1992; Janicki, 1989). Regarding life expectancy of adults with cerebral palsy, an earlier age-specific mortality can be expected. Older adults with cerebral palsy may exhibit an increasing rate of impairment in motor and sensory abilities along with a range of problems that appear to be more idiosyncratic, thus serving to differentiate members of this population in old age (Overeynder, Turk, Dalton, & Janicki, 1992). Cerebral palsy, like Down syndrome, may be a disability that poses challenges associated with discriminating among the effects of the aging process, pathological aging, preventable secondary conditions, and primary disability.

In summary, the health and functional status of older persons with developmental disabilities is an area in which research evidence continues to underscore the importance of targeting the maintenance of skills in individuals as they age. The primary means by which skills are maintained is the promotion of activity involvement in the following areas: physical health and fitness, psychological adjustment and health, major life activity (vocational/retirement, leisure/recreation, community involvement), and socialization and social support. Two model service areas are introduced below, in brief, as illustrative of age-appropriate, normative activity for promoting the health, fitness, and quality of life for aging adults with developmental disabilities.

PHYSICAL AND PSYCHOLOGICAL HEALTH AND FITNESS

Physical. Several conditions (e.g., decreased muscle strength, increased body fat, reduced flexibility, and loss of stamina) are often mistakenly attributed to aging rather than a direct result of sedentary lifestyle (Kultgen & Holtz, 1992). Research on the general older adult population, however, has documented the effects of exercise participation on slowing or reversing losses of function in various areas of physical performance. These areas also are directly related to the onset and progress of disease states. Circulation, blood pressure, bone density, cholesterol levels, control of weight, and energy reserves are all amenable to improvement via carefully designed and implemented exercise programs. Flexibility can be enhanced, if not remediated; muscle strength can be regained, if not improved; and cardiovascular function can be preserved through a regular program of physical activity.

Peggy Holtz has designed a program of physical fitness activity that has been specifically developed to accommodate the needs of older adults, with and without developmental disabilities, who are participants in a community-based adult activities program. This program focuses upon design elements (e.g., frequency, intensity, and duration; and motivational strategies), warm up strategies, strengthening activities, cardiovascular activities, and cool down strategies.

Psychological. Equally important to physical health and fitness is the psychological well-being of the adult who is aging. Age-sensitive program planning will focus on the prevention of unnecessary decline in the psychological functioning of the individual (Kultgen & Holtz, 1992). Two particular areas emerge in this process: (a) the maintenance of cognitive skills to the highest degree possible, and (b) the promotion of emotional well-being.

Jane Harlan has developed a model creative art experiences program to address the psychological health and adaptation of aging adults with developmental disabilities (Harlan, 1992). As these individuals experience the social-emotional, physical, and cognitive changes common in older adulthood, they may need support in understanding and adjusting to them. Emotional losses (e.g., death of family members or friends, or the departure of a roommate), physical changes (e.g., graying hair, vision or hearing losses), or changes in life activity (e.g., retirement) all may have a serious impact on the psychological well-being of the aging adult with developmental disabilities.

The creative art model was designed to focus on the use of creativity and art materials for the purpose of providing opportunities to communicate feelings, enhance self-esteem, and strengthen one's identity, especially as it relates to empowerment for self-determination. Communication, cognitive and manual skill development, self-esteem building, the promotion of autonomy, and the facilitation of social interaction are critical building blocks of the model. The goal of these activities is enhanced emotional, mental, and physical well-being of the individual.

CONCLUSION

In research by Hawkins and associates (Hawkins, 1993; Hawkins, 1991; Hawkins, Eklund, & Martz, 1992), age was shown to have a significant negative relationship with both involvement in activity and perceived satisfaction with life by aging adults with mental retardation. Activity involvement, however, has been shown to be directly linked with health and functional status in older adulthood. The same research by Hawkins et al. suggests that adults with mental retardation will indicate preferences and interest in activity involvement in older adulthood. Their level of adaptive skill maintenance also suggests that they have the capability for involvement in a broad range of physically and psychologically active pursuits. From this research, then, we might deduce that adults with developmental disabilities constitute a target population for therapeutic recreation specialists' attention.

The therapeutic recreation specialist has the appropriate level of professional preparation to understand the program development and leadership strategies needed to promote happy, fit, well-adjusted, and involved lifestyles for older adults with developmental disabilities. Facilitating the inclusion of these individuals into the mainstream of recreational programs will be a stimulating opportunity for therapeutic recreation specialists to bridge the developmental disabilities network with the aging services network, as well as with the recreation network.

AUTHOR NOTE

The author holds a Doctorate in Recreation from Indiana University, a Master of Science degree from the University of Montana and a Bachelor of Science degree from the University of New Hampshire in Recreation and Park Administration. Dr. Hawkins has professional experience in activity programming for older adults with disabilities, especially in health promotion, fitness, and leisure education. She specializes in lifespan development, and developmental disabilities, and leisure behavior. She has received numerous federal and state grants to study the special concerns of aging adults with mental retardation and other developmental disabilites. She has served as President of the Leisure and Recreation Division, and two terms as a member of the Board of Directors of the American Association on Mental Retardation. Also, Dr. Hawkins has served as President of the Society of Park and Recreation Educators, and Vice Chair of the Special Interest Group on Aging/MR in the Gerontological Society of America. She is co-author of a new book, *Therapeutic Activity Intervention with the Elderly: Foundations and Practices*, published by Venture Publishing. She is the author of numerous research articles and book chapters on aging and developmental disabilities.

REFERENCES

Brown, M.C., Bontempo, A., & Turk, M. (1991). *Secondary consequences of cerebral palsy: Adults with cerebral palsy in New York State.* Albany, NY: New York State Office of Mental Retardation and Developmental Disabilities.

Harlan, J.E. (1992). *A guide to setting up a creative art experiences program for older adults with developmental disabilities.* Bloomington, IN: Indiana University Institute for the Study of Developmental Disabilities–A University Affiliated Program.

Hawkins, B.A. (1993). An exploratory analysis of leisure and life satisfaction in aging adults with mental retardation. *Therapeutic Recreation Journal, 27*(2), 98-109.

Hawkins, B.A., Eklund, S.J., & Martz, B.L. (1992). *Detecting aging-related declines in adults with developmental disabilities: A research monograph.* Cincinnati, OH: Rehabilitation Research and Training Center Consortium on Aging and Developmental Disabilities.

Janicki, M.P. (1989). Aging, cerebral palsy, and older persons with mental retardation. *Australia and New Zealand Journal of Developmental Disabilities, 15*(3,4), 311-320.

Kultgen, P., & Holtz, P. (1992). *Age change and what to do about it.* Bloomington, IN: Indiana University Institute for the Study of Developmental Disabilities–University Affiliated Program.

Overeynder, J., Turk, M., Dalton, A.J., & Janicki, M.P. (1992). *I'm worried about the future: The aging of adults with cerebral palsy.* Albany, NY: New York State Developmental Disabilities Planning Council.

Rudelli, R.D. (1985). The syndrome of musculoskeletal aging. In M.P. Janicki & H.M. Wisniewski (Eds.), *Aging and developmental disabilities: Issues and approaches (pp. 229-256).* Baltimore, MD: Paul H. Brookes.

Siegel, J. (1976). *Demographic aspects of aging and the older population in the United States* (CPS, Special Studies, Series P-23, No. 59). Washington, DC: U.S. Government Printing Office.

Shock, N.W., Greulich, R.C., Costa, P.T., Andres, R., Lakata, E.G., Arenberg, D., and Tobin, J.D. (1984). *Normal human aging: The Baltimore longitudinal study of aging.* Washington, D.C.: NIH Publication No. 84-2450, Superintendent of Public Documents, U.S. Government Printing Office.

Chapter 3

Fitness and Exercise for Older Adults with Developmental Disabilities

Linda Bane Frizzell

The value of physical exercise for older adults has been well established by professionals in a variety of health-related fields. Current research confirms the fact that time stands still for no person. All of us will feel the results of aging regardless of physical condition, gender, or past and present physical activity level. Although the relative contributions of environment and genetics have yet to be clearly delineated, the average individual loses functional capacity at the rate of approximately 1 percent a year after age 30. However, this loss of functional ability is related to the general population and is not representative of the rate of aging for individuals who experience additional stresses everyday such as physical disabilities and reduced mental functioning. Thus, the value of physical exercise may have additional implications to the developmentally disabled older adult.

WHY DO OLDER ADULTS WITH DEVELOPMENTAL DISABILITIES NEED EXERCISE?

Few professionals have addressed the exercise needs of the older mentally impaired, diseased, or disabled adult. This factor is easily

---

Linda Bane Frizzell, PhD, is Tribal Health Planner, Leech Lake Reservation, Minnesota.

[Haworth co-indexing entry note]: "Fitness and Exercise for Older Adults with Developmental Disabilities." Frizzell, Linda Bane. Co-published simultaneously in *Activities, Adaptation & Aging* (The Haworth Press, Inc.) Vol. 21, No. 3, 1997, pp. 37-51; and: *Older Adults with Developmental Disabilities and Leisure: Issues, Policy, and Practice* (ed: Ted Tedrick) The Haworth Press, Inc., 1997, pp. 37-51. Single or multiple copies of this article are available for a fee from The Haworth Document Delivery Service [1-800-342-9678, 9:00 a.m. - 5:00 p.m. (EST). E-mail address: getinfo@haworth.com].

explained since the exercise needs of all older adults have only recently been considered. We as a society are starting to see an evolution in the acceptance of formal exercise for older adults, but this is only a beginning. While there are some established programs and a few "experts" in the field, there must continue to be emphasis placed on the importance of exercise for all older adults. The exercise programs need to be specific to the needs of older adult populations. These programs should strive to be comprehensive and motivate individuals to take care of their own well being.

Regular physical exercise is an important component for maintenance of physical and emotional well being, as evidenced by inclusion of exercise programs as an integral part of the care of institutionalized older adults. A main goal of these programs should be to maintain flexibility and strength that can reduce dependency and reduce the rate of physical deterioration. Individuals that do not require institutionalization should have goals and objectives similar to younger populations. These objectives should include an awareness of the importance of regular physical exercise as a preventive effect on the incidence and progression of chronic diseases. These are diseases that are often related to the aging process and are a result of increased prevalence of sedentary lifestyles.

Active people of all ages, both low and high intensity exercisers, have significantly lower coronary artery disease (CAD) than do sedentary individuals. Additionally, exercise plays an important role in the treatment of hypertension, obesity, hypercholesterolemia, myocardial infarction, and congestive heart failure (Goldfine, Ward, Taylor, Carlucci, & Rippe, 1991). Rikli and Edwards (1991) suggested that sedentary individuals can realize the benefits of exercise participation and significantly reverse certain motor (muscle) and cognitive declines in performance at almost any age. Further, exercise can benefit disabled persons who have lifestyles similar to the non-disabled population but who, because they have been burdened with a disability, are more likely to "age" faster (Kemp, 1983).

Exercise is known to preserve many physiological responses in the healthy elderly; yet, those with physical impairments are often discouraged from exercising (Thompson, Crist, March, & Rosenthal, 1988). McPhillips, Pellettera, Barret-Connor, Wingard, and

Criqui (1989) found that exercise frequency was lower in those with a history of chronic disease, obesity, or current cigarette smoking; yet exercise was positively associated with physical and emotional functioning and self-rated health.

While benefits can be achieved by all populations from exercise, perhaps the most important aspects of exercise are disregarded. These benefits are so basic to well-being that they are often overlooked and not considered to be a function related to physical activity levels. These benefits are: maintenance of stamina, improved appearance, ease of ingestion and elimination, better sleep, and especially important, the enthusiasm generated by the sensation of "feeling good."

BASIC GUIDELINES FOR DEVELOPMENT OF EXERCISE PROGRAMS

As a result of the pursuit and demand of exercise programs for older adults, recommendations and position statements have been written to ensure comprehensive development of safe programs. While there are not guidelines for developmentally disabled adults, these principles should be utilized as a minimum and additional assessments made to apply to the special needs of developmentally disabled older adults by the exercise director. The American Alliance for Health, Physical Education, Recreation and Dance Committee on Aging adopted several General Guidelines for Exercise Programs for Older Persons (age 50 and older):

1. Each participant in the program should be periodically monitored for signs of stress (unduly high heart rate, nausea, difficulty in breathing, pallor, or pain). Participants should be taught to monitor their own heart rate and to recognize and report irregularities to their exercise leader.
2. Every exercise program must have a well-defined emergency plan for exercise leaders to follow in case of cardiac arrest or other accidents.
3. Adequate supervision must be available for exercise programs. Exercise leaders should be trained in cardiopulmonary resuscitation techniques, or, at the very minimum, CPR-

trained personnel should be in close proximity to the exercise program (Penner, 1990).

In a position statement by the U.S. Centers for Disease Control and Prevention and the American College of Sports Medicine it is recommended that: *every adult should accumulate 30 minutes or more of moderate-intensity physical activity over the course of most days of the week.*

Two additional factors specific to developmentally disabled adults should also be considered when developing exercise programs. These are:

1. Use age appropriate equipment and language.
2. Protect against misleading some participants who may trust and agree to everything an authority figure asks.

USE QUALIFIED PERSONNEL TO DIRECT THE EXERCISE PROGRAM

It is strongly recommended that any exercise program be administered and programmed by a fully qualified exercise specialist. Failure to program and facilitate appropriate exercise regimens will result in frustration and sometimes injury by the participants. Administrators and communities planners that are interested in exercise programming should screen people who claim to be exercise specialists by asking to see their credentials and samples of their programs. Examples of appropriate qualifications are individuals with college degrees in exercise and sport sciences and/or certifications by organizations that have national level standards such as the American College of Sports Medicine and the American Council on Exercise. (Do not assume that medical or nursing staff are qualified to provide appropriate exercise programs.)

BEFORE STARTING AN EXERCISE PROGRAM

Before any older adult begins an exercise program, they should have a pre-exercise assessment of: current individual capabilities, limitations, personal and family health history, medications, and history of exercising activities. If, for example, during the pre-exercise assessment, it is determined that an individual is at risk to begin an exercise program such as, a family history of coronary artery disease or prescription medication that would affect physical performance. These would be examples that should be referred for a medical evaluation. Many exercise specialists will require medical approval before a patient/client begins an exercise program and some facilities will have protocols that must be followed for medical releases. It is important to safeguard against injury, learning the medical history and indications from a physical exam can aid in exercise programming.

Medical evaluations should include special attention to the cardiovascular, pulmonary, musculoskeletal, and neurologic systems. If the medical evaluation identifies disorders and limitations, further assessment is indicated to determine pathophysiologic severity and significance. Exercise is contraindicated in a very few situations, the two most common are post myocardial infarction and infections. For example, if coronary artery disease (CAD) exists, further assessment is required; a resting and exercise ECG may be needed to assist in exercise prescription. Other additional pre-exercise assessments for other predispositions may include laboratory tests such as urinalysis and counts of serum lipids, triglycerides, cholesterol, blood glucose, and blood cell. These assessments can also aid in determining the type of exercise program that should be initiated, either aerobic (high or low intensity), strength training, or isometric depending on the individual's health, level of fitness, physical abilities, and interests. Older adults, because of physical limitations and potential for physical problems, require more individualization of their exercise programs than do younger adults (Van Camp & Boyer, 1989).

CONSIDERATIONS FOR BASIC EXERCISE PROGRAMMING

Previously sedentary exercise participants must begin an exercise program slowly and, because the benefits of exercise appear to remain only as long as one continues to exercise, lifetime exercise participation is the goal (Dychtwald, 1986).

Participant adherence to an exercise program may be dependent on level of intensity. Because fitness can be attained and maintained at low intensity levels, experience with older adults indicates that lower intensity activities such as group exercises, tennis, walking, jogging, swimming, and badminton are more desired, in contrast to a high intensity cardiovascular fitness program (Wakat & Odom, 1982). Additionally, Wakat and Odom (1982) found that programs which focus on lifetime skills and stretch and balance types of activity are generally more effective in providing not only physiological improvements but also psychosocial benefits. Van Camp and Boyer (1989) concurred, reiterating that the elderly person's ability to attain a sufficiently high exercise intensity is the least important factor in a successful program and should not be overemphasized. Programs limited to cardiovascular fitness are valuable and desirable for some individuals but do not always provide for more than physiological improvement (Wakat & Odom, 1982). Cardiovascular endurance can be achieved at lower intensity levels by maintaining the exercise for a longer duration (Monahan, 1987). This enables the exercisers to regulate their own intensity safely and improve cardiovascular fitness.

Exercise programming for the diseased and disabled older adult must be diverse, as this population has many special needs. Kemp (1983) states that disabled persons have frequently lacked strenuous physical exercise as a result of being disabled. As a consequence, these individuals have not developed cardiac and respiratory reserves. Exercise can be an important factor to improving physical fitness and thus promoting life satisfaction for disabled and handicapped older adults.

Before an exercise program is developed for an individual, it is helpful to consult with other health care providers who have provided hands on therapies with the patient/client. This helps to determine methods for stimulating movement, physical limitations, preferred approaches to therapy (e.g., touch sensitivities), and precautions to be taken to avoid mistrust. This knowledge can promote patient/client rapport and aid in compliance of a comprehensive exercise program for the developmentally disabled older adult.

Considerations for movement may be confounded for the developmentally disabled older adult that develops handicapping conditions related to aging including the following: blindness and partially sightedness, deafness and hard of hearing, increased reaction times, and other reduced sensory perceptions (e.g. thermal, pressure, smell, etc.). There are also various health-related problems such as asthma, diabetes, and seizure disorders, cardiac and respiratory deficiencies, stroke and other brain-related disorders, Alzheimer's disease, and multiple conditions found in various combinations that tend to occur as people age.

Prescribing exercise for those with handicapping conditions depends upon the participants' ability to understand and execute the correct motor command to a given stimulus. The type of specific handicap or illness and corresponding medication must be understood by the exercise specialist in order to provide an appropriate exercise prescription. Modification of exercise programs should be expected in order to provide for varying levels of skills and varying abilities to receive and interpret stimuli to produce a successful response (Leslie, 1989).

Older adults with mental impairments may require more time to become familiar with and understand exercise movements. Reid, Seidl, and Montgomery (1989) suggested that adequate time be given for familiarization with equipment, movement skill, and refamiliarization with the task during physical fitness testing. Individuals with common chronic diseases such as degenerative joint disease, hypertension, emphysema, hypothyroidism, diabetes mellitus, dizziness, and ataxia also require prescribed exercise programs that allow for individual adaptations to produce the desired response.

GOALS FOR DEVELOPING AN EXERCISE PROGRAM

The option of cardiovascular rehabilitation through exercise is often overlooked for elderly cardiac patients (Williams & Sketch, 1990). Some elderly persons fear sudden death as a result of exercising. Exercise-induced sudden death in individuals older than 40 years of age is almost always due to atherosclerosis, which is usually preceded by chest pain or discomfort or a history of cardiac events (Herbert & Froelicher, 1991). An exercise program can gradually help cardiac patients overcome anxiety if the program addresses not only physiological needs but also the patients' needs for reassurance, support, and contact with other people (Williams & Sketch, 1990).

Even elderly cardiac patients and patients on beta-blockers may accrue moderate physiological benefits from exercise, such as weight loss, reduced body fat, lowering of resting heart rate, and increased forced expiratory volume (FEV) (Williams & Sketch, 1990). Lonnerbland (1984) claimed that if physically passive patients can be persuaded to maintain muscle and joint function by adhering to a simple exercise program, their risk of becoming dependent and requiring institutionalization is lowered.

Many older adults including the general public function at near critical levels of physical dysfunction. Unfortunately, this dysfunction is not generally apparent until it is too late. This undetectable state is demonstrated by humans that practice life smoking, abusing drugs, being sedentary, or eating non-nutritious diets, resulting in what appears to be a sudden "break down." Examples of sudden breakdowns are: lung cancer, from years of smoking; heart disease from years of a sedentary lifestyle; or a broken hip from osteoporoses, a result of years of a diet low in calcium.

Many developmentally disabled adults may function at critical physical dysfunction levels due to: *institutionalization,* patients/clients are not encouraged to move because it is faster and easier for staff to perform daily cares; *protected care,* patient/client is discouraged from movement and has not been allowed to learn or experience independence; or *hidden care,* patient/client is kept out of the eye of the public or hidden in restrictive environments (not as prevalent as in the first part of the century).

It is important for life satisfaction in all stages of life for an individual to practice life in an environment that is conducive to movement and has stimulations that make movement enjoyable. Thus, psychological influences will weigh strongly on adherence to an active lifestyle. Some of the benefits that affect individual motivation to lead active lifestyles are:

1. individuals feel better about themselves
2. increases autonomy

3. promotes initiative taking
4. promotes positive comments
5. increases social interaction
6. enhances self-image

Exercise programs must be designed for the present functioning level of the participants, and have goals that are achievable and realistic. Successful feedback is vital as a basis to build trust and perception of competence in physical activity. If an individual does not experience some level of success (does not need to be totally successful) it is difficult to convince that individual to continue to exercise. Exercise programs should always start with a movement that will result in a successful or positive attempt by the patient/client. After the patient/client has experienced an initial success then progress to more difficult movements or extend the length of exercise time. An individual's rate of progression will be reflected by the ability of the participant(s) to maintain an element of success in their exercise experience.

Exercise programming may need to be very individualized, dependent upon clientele, which may or may not have the ability to show an improvement in physical fitness. Exercise programs are also valuable in that they provide for maintenance of current movement, especially for the very old. The maintenance of movement and strength by the very old should be considered an improvement due to the non-reversible effects of aging. Thus, exercise programs for very old populations should be concerned with preserving flexibility and strength needed to maximize personal independence for daily cares.

EXAMPLES OF BASIC EXERCISE PROGRAMS
FOR DEVELOPMENTALLY DISABLED OLDER ADULTS

Group Exercise: Giant Beach Ball Game

(Note: generally beach balls are accepted as appropriate for all ages, if the term "Beach Ball" is a problem for age appropriate guidelines in some states, the term "Therapeutic Ball" can be substituted.)

The participants are seated in a large circle with the exercise leader and other staff in the center to provide visual and verbal reinforcement. Every exercise period should began with a five-minute warm-up consisting of static stretching of arms, legs, back, and neck. Participants who require assistance in moving limbs can be assisted by staff using a passive range of motion (PROM) technique to ensure readiness for exercise. Explain to the participants why they are stretching.

The game uses 2 large multicolored lightweight vinyl 4' diameter beach balls. (The lightweight ball is used to protect participants who do not have fast reaction times or do not or can not respond to the action of smaller harder balls that are difficult to visually perceive before contact is made.) Participants can be bumped by this ball and not sustain injuries. The participants are encouraged to throw, punch, push, or hit with their head, shoulder, knee, or foot the two 4' balls around the circle to other participants or staff. There is only one rule to the game: *everyone must remain seated.* If the balls go out of the circle, they should be retrieved by a staff person. The participants should receive verbal encouragement and acknowledgment every time they touch the ball. No movement is judged to be "bad." Participants' names can be used as additional reinforcement and recognition when they actively attempt any participation in the game. The size and colors of the balls can be visually stimulating for participants and will sometimes activate a reflexive response to participate when the ball is directed toward them.

Goals:

- Provide an enjoyable movement experience.
- Maintain or improve flexibility.
- Stimulate sensory responses.
- Stimulate reflexive responses.

Keys for optimum participation:

1. Remind the participants that it is "okay" to have fun. Some older adults have been lead to believe that they are too old to have fun.

2. Let the balls hit the staff in the center of the circle, this tends to amuse the participants and can stimulate greater participation efforts.
3. Ensure that all participants are given a chance to touch the balls. Staff can direct the balls close to those who do not have the flexibility to reach and strike the ball.
4. The enthusiasm level of the staff will be reflected in the efforts of the participants. Staff should be *constantly* reinforcing the attempts of the participants.

Group or Individual Exercise: Exer-Band Exercises

Group can be seated in a circle or in rows, caution against placing chairs too close to restrict movement. Began with a five-minute warm-up consisting of static stretching of arms, legs, back, and neck. Participants who require assistance in moving limbs can be assisted by staff using a passive range of motion (PROM) technique to ensure readiness for exercise. Explain to the participants why they are stretching.

The participants use exercise stretch bands that can be made from surgical rubber tubing or rubber bands that are available commercially. Various sizes of rubber tubing/bands can be used, dependent upon the strength of the participants. The smaller diameter tubing should be used by participants who have low arm strength while the larger diameter tubing should be used by those who effortlessly stretch the small diameter tubing. The concept is to determine which size of tubing will allow movement and provide work for the muscles.

The exercise leader should visually and verbally demonstrate the use of the exercise bands in the center of the circle or in front of the single participant. In large groups other staff can provide individual instruction and assistance in understanding the use of the exercise bands. Some specific exercises are:

Lateral Arm Movement to strengthen back, shoulder, arm, and hand muscles: The participants should be verbally encouraged to stretch the exercise band as far as they can, holding the exercise band in front of their chest and moving their arms laterally outward. Encourage participant(s) to perform a minimum of one set of six repetitions. Participants that improve to perform a maximum of three sets of six repetitions can then gradually increase the number of repetitions in each set to a maximum of twelve. Participants that can perform three sets of twelve repetitions should be upgraded to a thicker exercise band. Partially paralyzed participants may be included in the group by fastening the exercise tube/band end to either their foot or wheelchair bracket.

Pressing Movement to strengthen shoulder, arm, and hand muscles: The participants should be verbally encouraged to do the single arm overhead press. Those who can use both arms and hands should hold one end of the exercise band at waist level and raise the other hand, palm facing out, pressing upward as far as possible over the head. Those who are not bilateral can hook the exercise band to their foot or wheelchair. Follow the same sets and repetitions protocol as the *Lateral Arm Movement*.

Arm Curling Movement to strengthen arm and hand: The participants should be verbally encouraged to do the single arm curl. Those who have use of both arms should alternate arms, in a curling motion upward, palm facing up. One end of the exercise tube/band is hooked on the foot or other position that is lower than the outreached arm. Follow the same sets and repetitions protocol as the *Lateral Arm Movement*.

Participants should be told that they can stop at any time if they feel too tired to continue or if the movement is too painful to participate.

Goals:

- Provide an enjoyable movement experience.
- Maintain or improve strength.
- Maintain or improve muscle tone for appearance.

Keys for optimum participation:

1. Put handles of plastic pipe or electrical conduit on the ends of the tubing to provide an easy grip. The plastic handles can range in size from 3/8" to 1" diameter to accommodate differing hand sizes and abilities to flex fingers due to arthritis or other functional difficulties.
2. Take time to determine starting strength of participants. Stretch bands that are too thick will cause participants to be-

come discouraged from continued participation because they are not perceiving success. Those that are given a stretch band that is too small will not work the muscles at a level to improve strength, only flexibility.

3. Other exercise movements can be added to strengthen various other muscle groups. Using the basic principles from the above exercises should allow adaptability to specific patient/client needs.

SUMMARY

The facilitation of an exercise program may require spontaneity. It is imperative that the exercise director be well versed in alternative methods of stimulating volunteer physical movement as well as realizing benefits of various levels of exercise participation. Success levels in exercise programs cannot always be gauged objectively. It should be understood that to some individuals the ability to voluntarily move one finger or support a smile may be a landmark accomplishment and may not be readily recognized by observation. It is important for the exercise staff that actually conduct the hands-on exercise routines, to understand their patients/clients. This will certainly involve learning non-traditional means of communicating and recognition of movement actions that will "speak" to the exercise leader to help facilitate beneficial and enjoyable exercises.

Short attention spans must be considered in allowing extra time to reintroduce exercises or movements over and over again. Methods of stimulating movement, using reflexive, proprioceptive, visual, or verbal cues should be considered as common procedures to be incorporated into a comprehensive exercise program, as well as precautions in dealing with maladaptive behaviors.

There may be other stimulating factors in an exercise setting that are unexplained and unobservable that may cause uncharacteristic behaviors and reactions by the exercise participants. Some patients/clients may become hyperactive and uncontrollable, others may participate in parallel movements but will not join the group to exercise, and some may become totally uninhibited, actively speaking and moving about freely. An exercise director should be aware of unexpected reactions from exercise activities and ensure that policies and procedures are in place to protect the safety of all participants.

A well designed exercise program can be used to promote the sense of movement that is inherent in human activity, to encourage the ability to respond, and to support or improve quality of life. Possibly older adults with developmental disabilities have not been encouraged strongly or convincingly enough to motivate them to enjoy the benefits of exercise. To be free to enjoy movement and its sense of well being is clearly related to physical condition, social expectations, exercise knowledge, and personal goals. Exercise programming based on facts and individual needs and abilities should be available for all older adults, including those with developmental disabilities.

AUTHOR NOTE

The author's endeavors have included a broad range of professional preparations dedicated to improvement of quality of life across the life span.

While her current pursuits have taken her into designing health care programs, she continues to develop exercise programs and advocate for programs that improve life satisfaction of older adults. She has designed equipment and presented programs across the country that address the unique needs of mentally impaired, diseased, and disabled older adults. Her publications include: "Promotional considerations for exercise and physical activity in mentally impaired, diseased, and disabled adults; Effects of an exercise program for mentally impaired older adults in a long-term care facility" (ERIC Documents) and a contributing author to *A Research Source Book and Bibliography in Aging and Health, Exercise, Recreation and Dance*, AAHPERD Publications.

REFERENCES

Dychtwald, K. (Ed.). (1986). *Wellness and health promotion for the elderly.* Rockville, MD: Aspen Publication.

Goldfine, H., Ward, A., Taylor, P., Carlucci, D., & Rippe, J. M. (1991). Exercising to health. *Physician and Sportsmedicine, 19*(6), 81-93.

Herbert, W. G., & Froelicher, V. F. (1991). Exercise tests for coronary and asymptomatic patients. *Physician and Sportsmedicine, 19*(2), 55-58, 62.

Kemp, B. (1983). Aging among the disabled: A neglected area. (ERIC Document Reproduction Service No. ED 239 444)

Leslie, D. (Ed.). (1989). *Mature stuff: Physical activity for the older adult.* Reston, VA: AAHPERD Publications.

Lonnerbland, L. (1984). Exercises to promote independent living in older patients. *Geriatrics, 39*(2), 93-101.

McPhillips, J. B., Pellettera, K. M., Barrett-Conner, E., Wingard, D. L., & Criqui, M. H. (1989). Exercise patterns in a population of older adults. *American Journal of Preventive Medicine, 5*(2), 65-72.

Monahan, T. (1987). Is activity as good as exercise? *The Physician and Sportsmedicine, 15*(10), 181-186.

Penner, D. (1989). *Elder Fit.* Reston, VA: AAHPERD Publications.

Reid, G., Seidl, D., & Montgomery, P. L. (1989). Fitness tests for retarded adults. *JOPERD,* (8), 76-78.

Rikli, R. E., & Edwards, D. J. (1991). Effects of a three-year exercise program on motor function and cognitive processing speed in older women. *Research Quarterly for Exercise and Sport, 62*(1), 61-67.

Thompson, R. F., Crist, D. M., Marsh, M., & Rosenthal, M. (1988). Effects of physical exercise for elderly patients with physical impairments. *Journal of the American Geriatrics Society, 36,* 130-135.

Van Camp, S. P., & Boyer, J. L. (1989). Cardiovascular aspects of aging (part 1 of 2). *The Physician and Sportsmedicine, 17*(4), 121-130.

Van Camp, S. P., & Boyer J. L. (1989). Exercise guidelines for the elderly (part 2 of 2). *The Physician and Sportsmedicine, 17*(5), 83-88.

Wakat, D., & Odum, S. (1982). The older woman: Increased psychosocial benefits from physical activity. *JOPERD, 53*(3), 34-35.

Williams, M. A., & Sketch, M. H. (1990). After a heart attack, prescribing exercise to speed recovery. *Senior Patient, 1*(9), 16-20.

Chapter 4

Expressive Arts Programming for Older Adults Both With and Without Disabilities: An Opportunity for Inclusion

Diane B. Barret
Claire B. Clements

The beneficial effects of involvement with the arts on adults who are aging is well documented by researchers in the fields of arts education, aging, and disabilities. Bloom (1980) notes more positive attitudes and increased life satisfaction among elderly individuals who participated in creative arts experiences. Clements (1994) focuses on benefiting seniors through peer interaction and inclusion into community-based arts programs. Goff (1992) documents increases in flexible thinking among older adults who were given

Diane B. Barret, EdD, is Creative Arts Director, *Wellness Express: Arts/Fitness Intervention for Older Adults,* University Affiliated program for Persons with Developmental Disabilities, University of Georgia, 850 College Station Road, Athens, GA 30602.

Claire B. Clements, EdD, is Associate Professor, Staff Development and Technical Assistance Coordinator, Director, Aging Initiative and Arts Initiative, University Affiliated program for Persons with Developmental Disabilities, University of Georgia, 850 College Station Road, Athens, GA 30602.

[Haworth co-indexing entry note]: "Expressive Arts Programming for Older Adults Both With and Without Disabilities: An Opportunity for Inclusion." Barret, Diane B., and Claire B. Clements. Co-published simultaneously in *Activities, Adaptation & Aging* (The Haworth Press, Inc.) Vol. 21, No. 3, 1997, pp. 53-63; and: *Older Adults with Developmental Disabilities and Leisure: Issues, Policy, and Practice* (ed: Ted Tedrick) The Haworth Press, Inc., 1997, pp. 53-63. Single or multiple copies of this article are available for a fee from The Haworth Document Delivery Service [1-800-342-9678, 9:00 a.m. - 5:00 p.m. (EST). E-mail address: getinfo@haworth.com].

53

an opportunity to think creatively through the arts. Results of the Barret (1992) study underscored the validity of designing creative art experiences to foster self-expression among older adults, and the effectiveness of encounters with art in allowing older individuals to access other world views and to reflect upon their own. Research by Katz and Katz (1991) shows that adults with disabilities when exposed to quality arts programming can make significant achievements. Harlan (1993) points to improvement in the emotional health of individuals with disabilities through involvement in an expressive art program.

Given the value of providing older adults with opportunities for creative expression issues arise which must be addressed: (1) how does one design and implement a quality arts program, and (2) what needs to be considered when including older persons with disabilities in community-based programs?

Obviously, there are many answers to both of these questions. *The Arts/Fitness Quality of Life Activities Program,* Clements (1994), provides a well tested model for developing arts programs for senior adults both with and without disabilities. Basic to the design of each lesson is the Incubation Model of Creativity (Torrance, 1990), which includes the before, during, and after stages. The strength of the model is that it emphasizes the importance of motivation as a springboard for creativity, it provides sequential ideas for the actual hands-on studio activity, and then sets aside time for reflection, dialogue, and group sharing. Suggestions for carrying the experience into the lives of participants are included as an important part of the final stage. The discipline based approach to art education espoused by the Getty Foundation (1985) is also incorporated into the design of many art lessons. This model stresses the importance of involving participants in aesthetic interaction, critical dialogue, art historical learning, as well as hands-on art activities in order to enrich their total experience.

OVERCOMING ATTITUDINAL BARRIERS

One of the greatest challenges in developing an expressive arts program is that of attitudinal barriers. Many older adults believe that they lack creative ability, so they are more comfortable working from established patterns or copying (Greenberg, 1985). Asking a group to generate their own images and ideas can trigger a great deal of fear and uncertainty. It is important to create a safe environment which is non judgmental and encourages risk taking. Some strategies for helping participants move through this initial phase include:

1. Encouragement, encouragement, encouragement! Find ways to give positive feedback which is genuine.
2. Accept each person where they are developmentally and then help them to see their own improvement.
3. Join in yourself. Let the group see that you are willing to expose yourself and take risks.
4. Ease the group into creative projects by designing a series of experiences which gradually involve more personal investment and which build skill levels.
5. Try a variety of media and approaches such as clay, photography, collage, puppetry, painting on an unusual surface, and group projects. Beware of drawing on paper with real novices who generally equate artistic ability with representational skills. They may feel so unsuccessful that they will be discouraged from trying anything else.
6. Spend time planning your art activity. The more energy you put into gathering motivational materials and thinking through the entire sequence of experiences the more effective the lesson will be.
7. Design lessons which build on areas of strength within your group of older adults. Find something that they already are good at or are interested in as a theme for the art lesson.

Lepore and Janicki (1990) provide this quote from staff at a demonstration site where older persons with disabilities were included in community aging programs: "Seniors with developmental disabilities are usually cheerful and enthusiastic about program activities which contributes in a beneficial way to the collective good spirits of the whole group"(p. 25). This positive attitude can also enhance an arts program where many senior adults are fearful of failure or of self disclosure.

PROVIDING OPTIMUM ENVIRONMENTS
FOR ALL PEOPLE

In addressing the question, "how can older persons both with and without disabilities be successfully included in community programs?" consider the following:

A new time and movement is with us, and it has been called the era of community membership, characterized by an emphasis on functional supports to enhance community integration, quality of life and individualization (Knoll, 1992). The day of building separate arts programming for people with developmental disabilities is over. The most beneficial settings for many people with disabilities to participate in the arts are community-based programs (Clements, 1994). Community-based means programs that already exist and are operational in the community. Part of the reason these provide a fine vehicle for people with disabilities who are interested in the arts and in self expression is because arts classes tend to have a non-judgmental, secure atmosphere, which is necessary to foster creativity. Today people with disabilities, in many states, are exercising their rights to choose from an array of community arts programs. As providers of programs in the arts, it is our responsibility to understand how and what to do to promote positive inclusive, arts experiences. Not only should these programs be designed to facilitate the growth and development of the creativity of participants, but simultaneously they should contribute to happiness and complement social growth. By using basic guidelines, people with disabilities can be enabled to participate to their fullest potential, interacting with their peers who do not have disabilities.

Guideline #1: Explore how and where, in your community, the arts can provide vehicles for inclusion of people with disabilities.

1. Analyze the community to determine if there are already existing arts programs in places such as the "Y," community agencies, departments of recreation, places of worship, schools, universities, and private organizations that would be good settings for inclusion.

Guideline #2: Explore ways to assess the suitability of each program to conduct inclusive arts programming. Questions to consider are:

1. Is the administration receptive to fostering the inclusion of people with disabilities in the regular programming?
2. What experiences have the program participants previously had with people with disabilities? Were they positive or negative?
3. Are participants willing to providing a nurturing environment in which to include people with disabilities?
4. Is the staff prepared to adapt and make programming accessible for people with disabilities? If not, explore avenues to arranging this training.

Guideline #3: Provide in-service training for staff in community-based settings. Through staff training and working with seniors, ways to provide successful inclusive community programming can become a reality. This approach maximizes the impact of what is already available in each community.

In addition to taking a look at the programmatic suitability of community-based settings, consider the suitability of the program to promote social inclusion, as it is put forth by Blaney and Freud (1994) in their definition of social inclusion relating to recreation and leisure.

Does the programming occur with enough frequency to make a positive difference in the lives of people with disabilities?

Is the intensity of the interactions between people with and without disabilities enough to be of significance for people with disabilities?

Will the person with the disability be equal to the person without a disability? Will the relationship promote equality as in usual adult to adult interactions?

Will the person with the disability be able to give to the person without the disability?

The funding of a Project of National Significance by the Administration on Developmental Disabilities, called The Quality of Life/ Arts Fitness Program for Older People with and Without Developmental Disabilities provided the nucleus for the development of a cluster of community-based, inclusive arts programs. Discussions of two of these programs follow.

IMPORTANT PEOPLE–
A CASE STUDY
OF AN INCLUSIVE ARTS PROGRAM
BASED ON THE QUALITY OF LIFE MODEL

The Georgia University Affiliated Program (UAP) which is funded by HHS, the Administration on Developmental Disabilities, has an Arts Initiative. Under this arts umbrella falls The Quality of Life Project, an arts/fitness intervention, created and directed by UAP's Dr. Claire Clements between 1988 and 1991 which spawned a number of interesting programs. One such project, based on the Quality of Life museum component, is *Important People*, a museum outreach program for senior adults both with and without disabilities. Directed by Dr. Diane Barret and funded through the Grassroots Arts Grant Program of the Georgia Council for the Arts, the project was designed to coincide with an exhibition of photographs of well known African Americans held at the Georgia Museum from January 24-March 13, 1994. Senior adults from Hope Haven School and the Athens/Clarke County senior center were invited to participate in the four phase program.

Phase I

A pre-museum slide/lecture presentation at the Athens/Clarke County Senior Center whetted the interest of fifteen participants in the art of photography. They examined antique cameras, looked at photographs taken in the late 1800s and early 1900s, and discussed the evolution of photography as an art form. Photographs taken by Dorothea Lange during the depression years sparked a great deal of conversation. One senior adult reminisced about her mother's garden and its importance to their family during the depression. Another fondly remembered the sweet potato biscuits her mother had made to save on flour during those lean years. A photograph of Mary McLeod Bethune from the *Generations In Black and White* exhibition was examined to prepare the group for the museum field trip, and then everyone shared old family photos which individuals had brought to the lecture. During the final few minutes of the session participants were given the opportunity to become a photographer and take Polaroid snapshots of each other.

Phase II

The following Wednesday the group met at the Georgia Museum of Art for a guided tour through the exhibition *Generations In Black and White: Photographs by Carl Van Vechten from the James Weldon Johnson Memorial Collection.* Folding camp stools provided comfortable seating as participants viewed black and white photographs of African Americans who had made a tremendous variety of contributions to our culture. Listening to a tape of Bessie Smith, the "Empress of the Blues," singing "A'int Nobody's Business If I Do" brought smiles and started everyone's feet tapping. The group listened to an awe-inspiring breadth of musical contributions from Mahalia Jackson's rendition of "Take My Hand Precious Lord" to Ella Fitzgerald's "Take the A Train." One older man was moved to get up and start dancing to the rhythms of music by Dizzie Gillespie. Older adults not only viewed portraits of poets and writers of the Harlem Renaissance such as Zora Neale Hurston and Langston Hughes, but they heard them speak through their writings. At the end of the tour, everyone had feasted on a banquet of music, poetry, humor, and had learned a great deal about contributions made by distinguished people in the African American community.

Phase III

In order to extend this experience into their lives, senior participants were asked to become photographers themselves. A few weeks after viewing the exhibition of photography, the group was brought back together at the senior center and each person was given a disposable camera. This was the first time many of them had actually used a camera and they were delighted at the prospect. The mechanics of how to turn on the flash, which button to push, and how to aim the camera were of initial concern. There was a great deal of laughter as the group practiced on one another. After discussing such issues as proper lighting and good composition, everyone was given a camera to take home with the assignment of photographing important people in their lives. Several wanted to know if it would be permissible to take snapshots of pets who were special to them. This question revealed the importance of animals in the lives of many older people.

Phase IV

In the final phase of the project, cameras were collected, film developed, and participants were asked to select one photograph which they felt best captured the image of their "important person." A wide variety of subjects included children, great-grandchildren, ministers, friends, pets, center staff, and hairdressers. Volunteers worked with elders, taping their commentaries and helping them write a narrative description to accompany the photographs. An exhibition of these photographic images/commentaries was held in May at the Georgia Center in conjunction with the UAP's *Community Collection* of artwork. This annual exhibition brings together works of art by Georgians both with and without disabilities. The exhibition gave viewers access to the artistic expression of these elders as well as a knowledge of meaningful people in their lives.

Important People was a project that had a number of goals: (1) to raise participants' level of awareness of significant contributions made by a large number of African Americans, (2) to include senior adults both with and without disabilities in a creative arts program, (3) to allow participants to learn about photography as an art form and to express themselves through this medium, and (4) to honor older adults by saying to them: "You are important! We want to know more about you, and we want you to be involved in community cultural events."

THE COMMUNITY COLLECTION

Community Collection is a vehicle for the dissemination of visual and performing arts. Originated by Claire Clements, the event is a training site that provides gainful employment for students who conduct the event in its entirety, from sending out the invitations to returning the packages at the end of the exhibition. This annual exhibition provides an arena for showcasing and sharing the arts by people with and without disabilities. Exhibitors and performers are from throughout the state. The opening reception attracts 150 people and has featured such performers as a flutist without vision who was accompanied by a sighted pianist, a marimba soloist, and a fitness group whose members are with and without disabilities. Each year the exhibition has grown and averages about 130 entries with 70 works by over 50 artists that are displayed in highly visible spaces. Works are judged by museum educators, curators, artists from the region and by panels of people knowledgeable in the arts and in disabilities. The last two years there has been an exhibition by older people within the Community Collection show. The types of work vary, such as collaborative ceramic tile pieces, photography, videos, collages, painting, drawings and stitchery. Most of the works are quite personal showing that art transcends limitations, pushing them aside so that the act of creativity can take place. Each year a few works are purchased to add to the Community Collection. When inquiries are made to purchase a piece, the community member is encouraged to contact the artist directly. Together they decide the particulars of the sale. This activity further connects artists with the community on a very individual basis. The head of a large national corporation saw the works and inquired about purchasing works of art. When he learned, much to his surprise, that the works were done by people with disabilities, his corporation became the primary sponsor of the exhibit.

The works have been exhibited in prestigious spaces. For example, the UAP collaborated with the Mental Health Association and the Alliance for the Mentally Ill and in 1993 held an exhibition and premier performance at the Carter Center of Emory University in Atlanta. Again, in 1995 collaborating with the Mental Health Association, works were exhibited in Dublin, Ireland.

The programs discussed in this article were designed specifically to be vehicles for inclusion of people with developmental disabilities into community-based programs. There have been many lessons learned from the participants in each program. As we strive to meet the needs of each community member we learn what to do and how to make the next program better.

AUTHOR NOTE

Diane Barret received her EdD in art education from the University of Georgia in 1992 specializing in art for older adults. Over the past four years she has served on the staff of UGA's University Affiliated Program, directing the creative arts portion of *Wellness Express*, an arts/fitness project for older adults in rural counties. She has also directed senior outreach programs from the Goergia Museum of Art and is project director for "Singing Quilts," a 1996 Georgia Folklife/Humanities project with a strong intergenerational focus.

Dr. Barret has published numerous articles and is the author of the art and museum components of the recently published *Arts/Fitness Quality of Life Activities Program*. She coordinated the national Quality of Life visual arts teleconference broadcast from the Georgia Center for Continuing Education on September 29, 1994, and has been an invited speaker at aging and art conferences on state, regional, and national levels. She currently serves as Chairman of the Lifelong Learning Affiliate of the National Art Education Association.

Claire Clements authored and directed *Quality of Life, An Expressive Arts/ Physical Fitness Innovative Training/Research/Service Program for People who are Older*, a Project of National Signifigance grant awarded from the U.S. Department of HHS, Administration on Developmental Disabilities. For her HHS, Administration on Aging, grant award: "Quality of Life: A Series of Nationwide Aging and Arts Therapies Interactive Video Teleconferences," she received the National University Continuing Education Association, Division of Educational Telecommunication's 1995 Program of Excellence Award. She received the AAMR/Gerontological Society of America Special Interest Group on Aging's "1996 Special Interest Group on Aging Professional Leadership Award." With her colleagues, Clements wrote *Arts/Fitness, Quality of Life Activities Program: Creative Ideas for Working with Older Adults in Group Settings*, Health Professions Press.

REFERENCES

Barret, D. (1992) *Art and myth: A doorway in the world view of African American elders.* Doctoral dissertation, University of Georgia.

Bloom, L. (1980) Toward an understanding of lifelong growth and participation in visual arts production. In Hoffman, D. H., Greenberg, P. and Fitzner, D. (Eds.), *Lifelong learning and the visual arts* (pp. 78-97). Reston, Va: National Arts Education Association.

Blaney, B. C. & Freud, E. L. (1994).Trying to play together: Competing paradigms in approaches to inclusion through recreation and leisure in Bradley, V.

J., Ashbaugh, J. W., & Blaney, B. C. (Eds.) (1994). *Creating individual supports for people with developmental disabilities: A mandate for change at many levels.* (pp. 237-253). Baltimore, MD: Paul H. Brooks Publishing Co.

Clements, C. (1994). *The arts/fitness quality of life activities program* (pp. 5-14). Baltimore Md.: Health Professions Press, Inc.

Goff, K. (1992). Enhancing creativity in older adults. *The Journal of Creative Behavior,* 26(1), 40-49.

Greenberg, P. (1985) Senior citizens and art education. *School Arts,* 84(7), 38-40.

Harlan, J. E. (1992). *A Guide to Setting up A Creative Art Experiences Program for Older Adults with Developmental Disabilities.* Bloomington, Ind: Indiana University, Institute for the Study of Developmental Disabilities.

J. Paul Getty Trust. (1985). *Beyond creating: The place for art in America's schools.* Los Angeles, CA: Author.

Kaye, A., Sullivan, E. N., Benedict, M. A., Knoll, J., and Skowyra, D. (1994, May). *Aging and developmental disabilities in Michigan: A curriculum resource packet.* Lansing, MI: Aging and developmental Disabilities Project, Lansing Community College Section III.A. p 1.

Katz, F. L. & Katz, E. (1987). *Freedom to create.* Richmond, CA: National Institute of Art and Disabilities.

Lepore, P. & Janicki, M. P., 1990, *The wit to win: How to integrate older persons with developmental disabilities into community aging programs.* New York State Office for the Aging pp. 25, 35.

Torrance, E. P., & Safter, H. T. (1990). *The incubation model of teaching: Getting beyond the aha!* Buffalo, NY: Bearly Limited.

Chapter 5

Enriching Later Life Experiences for People with Developmental Disabilities

Evelyn Sutton

At the present time, the longevity of people who have lifelong (developmental) disabilities is an assured fact. These individuals, over 90% of whom are diagnosed with mental retardation, are living into their 60s, 70s, even 90s, a phenomenon that has come as a surprise to their families as well as to planners and service providers. The life history of many of these individuals is one of lengthy institutionalization. For some there were no guidelines such as IQ cutoffs at the time they entered the institution, and reasons for placement could vary from epilepsy, deafness, or incorrigibility to a true case of mental retardation. Institutional life did not include opportunities for education, vocational training or normal socialization, and those who were placed in institutions for reasons other than mental retardation, became functionally retarded as a result.

The institutions can only be described as a miserable environment, entirely discouraging to human growth and development. As a result of class action suits brought by families, conditions in the institutions have been greatly improved, and during the John F.

Evelyn Sutton, MA, is Senior Fellow and Adjunct Professor, Akron University's Institute for Life-Span Development and Gerontology.

[Haworth co-indexing entry note]: "Enriching Later Life Experiences for People with Developmental Disabilities." Sutton, Evelyn. Co-published simultaneously in *Activities, Adaptation & Aging* (The Haworth Press, Inc.) Vol. 21, No. 3, 1997, pp. 65-69; and: *Older Adults with Developmental Disabilities and Leisure: Issues, Policy, and Practice* (ed: Ted Tedrick) The Haworth Press, Inc., 1997, pp. 65-69. Single or multiple copies of this article are available for a fee from The Haworth Document Delivery Service [1-800-342-9678, 9:00 a.m. - 5:00 p.m. (EST). E-mail address: getinfo@haworth.com].

Kennedy administration, most of the residents were released into the mainstream to pursue the remainder of their lives. While some moved into a more or less successful independent lifestyle (Edgerton, 1995), the majority were placed in supervised group homes, nursing homes, or foster care, and became involved in sheltered workshops or other day programs sponsored by service provider agencies.

Now in their later years, concerns about their health, work, leisure activities and social networks have arisen. The past decade has seen an explosion in published research and practice approaches.

In 1984 researchers at The University of Akron investigated characteristics of 100 older adults with mental retardation and found them not too different in some ways from the great majority of older adults in the general population who are in good health and interested in pursuing active and productive later lives (Stroud & Sutton, 1988). Their deficits in social skills, social network, verbal abilities, literacy and community experience, however, set them apart from other "seniors."

With community inclusion and opportunities for new experiences as major goals, The University of Akron researchers also conducted a demonstration project under a grant from the Joseph P. Kennedy, Jr. Foundation. In this project, community volunteers from area churches and from the Retired Senior Volunteer Program (RSVP) were paired with older adults in the sheltered workshops. On a weekly basis they attended a variety of community sites such as museums, libraries, parks, senior centers, malls, etc., and enjoyed an outing together. Over a period of time, improvements in social skills, appearance, language, mood, motivation and general well-being were noted in the participants with the lifelong disability. Furthermore, the "pairs" became real friends in many cases (Roberts, Sutton & Miller, 1992).

In 1990, The University of Akron researchers began to investigate the status of older adults with mental retardation in terms of their work/retirement status, leisure activities, and preparation for later life, including retirement. Their study was largely limited to Ohio because that state had included the option to retire in its regulations addressing program needs of people with developmental disabilities. The aging and developmental disabilities service systems had also had a six year exposure to the research and training offered by The University of Akron. The researchers hypothesized that the older adults would have a choice of activities and pursuits representative of a traditional retirement lifestyle, and would also have some preparation for making decisions about lifestyle changes associated with later life.

Within their sample of 1,483 persons, they found well over half still at work (Sutton, Sterns, & Schwartz Park, 1993). Whether or not these older workers had been offered a retirement option was not clear. For those who were reportedly retired full or part time, the activity options available were not found to be innovative and consisted largely of crafts, musical activities, and group outings. Participation in community based senior centers, however, was more widespread than expected. Individualized programming was largely missing. Only 10% of the agencies surveyed reported any type of pre-retirement education for the older worker; some form of counseling was noted by a slightly larger percentage. But it was clearly a picture of here today and there tomorrow, a shifting of people around the system, sometimes dictated by the long lists of people waiting for admission to the service system.

In response to this finding, The University of Akron researchers, in collaboration with researchers at the University of Illinois at Chicago, developed the curriculum "Person-Centered Planning for Later Life." In its revised version, the curriculum presents 17 class sessions and 3 field trips with the purpose of helping the person understand later life options and learn how to make good decisions and choices. Staff and families associated with the individual in training are encouraged to provide "assisted autonomy" rather than planning *for* the person. This curriculum is now being widely used and becomes a basis for individualized planning and informed choice grounded in a knowledge of aging processes, realistic options for later life and choice-making opportunities.

Choice-making is a major focus of the curriculum. In addition to lessons that teach these concepts and skills, every lesson provides opportunities for practice. The participants make many choices during class time and report choices made between sessions. Between classes a designated "support person" within the residential or work setting, provides reinforcement in the concepts as well as further practice opportunities.

Consideration of later life and pre-retirement issues comes with lessons centering on health and wellness, free time activities, possible work schedule changes, friendships and support networks, community volunteering, and living arrangements. In final sessions class members identify goals for themselves and practice stating them at their service planning meetings.

An issue that sometimes arises among service providing professionals has to do with the extent to which habilitation and training goals must govern the activities of individuals as they grow older, since program funding is often based on such goals. It is now generally accepted that skill maintenance is acceptable as a later life goal. However, growth and development are to be encouraged whenever possible, with exercise, sensory stimulation, art, drama, appropriate crafts, horticulture, health and nutrition education, music appreciation, community exploration, volunteer work, and other community-based activities all possible frames of reference.

It has been widely noted that the current cohort of older people with mental retardation or other developmental disabilities often choose to continue working into their late 60s and 70s, or until physical decline forces them to make a change. This preference may reflect their relatively brief work histories, during which they have experienced satisfaction in productivity, work place socialization and earned discretionary income, however small. Deinstitutionalized in the late 70s, they went through placements, adjustments, training and, finally, sheltered work. Very few have had the opportunity for community employment. They perceive the value of work not only to their own well-being, but as the essence of society's esteem.

Opportunities for phase down, part time or continuation of work may be more available to this group of older adults than to those in the general population at least to the degree that the service system is flexible and attempts to individualize its services. In so doing, however, it must be assured that the person will participate in the decision to modify his/her work schedule or give up work altogether in favor of new experiences and leisure activities about which he or she has full knowledge and information.

AUTHOR NOTE

The author is co-editor and contributing author of *Older Adults with Developmental Disabilities: Optimizing Choice and Change* (Paul Brookes Publishing, 1993). Her research interests have focused on aging and developmental disabilities with a special concern for retirement planning; "Person-Centered Planning for Later Life" is a model curriculum she helped to develop. Ms. Sutton directed a demonstration project which paired non-disabled seniors with older adults having developmental disabilities in a variety of integrated settings.

She edits "A/DDvantage" a newsletter for the Rehabilitation Research and Training Center Consortium on Aging and Developmental Disabilities.

REFERENCES

Ansello, E. & Eustis, N. (Eds.) (1992). *Aging and Disabilities: Seeking Common Ground.* Amityville, NY, Baywood Publishing Co.

Edgerton, R., & Gaston, M. (1991). *I've Seen It All.* Baltimore, MD, Paul H. Brookes Publishing Co.

Roberts, R., Sutton, E., & Miller, S. (1992) *The Peer Companion Model.*

Seltzer, M., Krauss, M. & Janicki, M. (Eds.) (1994). *Life Course Perspectives on Adulthood and Old Age,* Annapolis, MD., AAMR Publication Center.

Stroud, M. & Sutton, E. (1988). *Expanding Options for Older Adults with Developmental Disabilities.,* Baltimore, MD., Paul H. Brookes Publishing Co.

Sutton, E., Heller, T., Sterns, H. L., Factor, A., & Miklos, S. (Eds.) (1994). *Person-Centered Planning for Later Life: A Curriculum for Adults with Mental Retardation.* Akron, Ohio, RRTC on Aging with Mental Retardation.

Sutton, E., Factor, A., Hawkins, B., Heller, T., & Seltzer, G., (Eds.) (1993). *Older Adults with Developmental Disabilities: Optimizing Choice and Change,* Baltimore, MD, Paul H. Brookes Publishing Co.

Sutton, E., Sterns, H.L., & Schwartz Park, L.S. (1993). Realities of retirement and pre-retirement planning. In E. Sutton, A. Factor, B. Hawkins, T. Heller, & G. Seltzer (Eds). *Older Adults with Developmental Disabilities: Optimizing Choice and Change, Baltimore,* MD: Park H. Brookes Publishing Co., pp. 95-106.

Chapter 6

Consumer Satisfaction for Individuals with Developmental Disabilities

Barbara Wilhite
Kathleen Sheldon

SUMMARY. Consumer satisfaction is a significant measure of the quality of service provision. Little information is available on consumer satisfaction for individuals with developmental disabilities, however. Information that is available may paint an overly optimistic view of the service system. Reasons for the tendency of service recipients to report high levels of satisfaction are presented. Suggestions for obtaining meaningful consumer satisfaction data are discussed. *[Article copies available from The Haworth Document Delivery Service: 1-800-342-9678. E-mail address: getinfo@haworth.com]*

The ultimate assurer of quality is the consumer. Consumer satisfaction is therefore a significant measure of the quality of service provision. Yet little information is available regarding consumer satisfaction for individuals with developmental disabilities. Perhaps

Barbara Wilhite, EdD, CTRS, is Recreation Coordinator, Department of Recreation and Leisure Studies, University of North Texas. Kathleen Sheldon is a doctoral student, Department of Recreation and Leisure Studies, the University of Georgia, Athens, GA.

[Haworth co-indexing entry note]: "Consumer Satisfaction for Individuals with Developmental Disabilities." Wilhite, Barbara and Kathleen Sheldon. Co-published simultaneously in *Activities, Adaptation & Aging* (The Haworth Press, Inc.) Vol. 21, No. 3, 1997, pp. 71-77; and: *Older Adults with Developmental Disabilities and Leisure: Issues, Policy, and Practice* (ed: Ted Tedrick) The Haworth Press, Inc., 1997, pp. 71-77. Single or multiple copies of this article are available for a fee from The Haworth Document Delivery Service [1-800-342-9678, 9:00 a.m. - 5:00 p.m. (EST). E-mail address: getinfo@haworth.com].

71

as a result, services tend to be oriented more to systems maintenance than to consumer preferences; geared more to staff than to
client characteristics (Morris & Harris, 1972).

Unfortunately, since attempts to determine consumer satisfaction
are often confined to known recipients, a "positive response bias"
can result (Berger, 1983). There are a variety of possible explana-
tions for this tendency to report very high levels of satisfaction.

Individuals who are receiving the service, by definition, must
like something about it. Those who respond to consumer satisfaction measures tend to be more satisfied than those who do not
respond. A vested interest in the service is not only important in
determining whether a survey is completed, but is also likely to
affect one's answers (Dillman, 1978). Recipients of services often
represent a self-selected group and are not necessarily those in
greatest need (Little, 1982).

Those in greatest need may be excluded from consumer satisfaction surveys because they are not designed with their needs in mind.
The limited abilities of some consumers may make it difficult to
respond to either a written or verbal survey. Consumers with developmental disabilities may have difficulty reading questions, understanding concepts, following directions, writing answers, or responding verbally. Dillman (1978) suggested that older people in
general were likely to be underrepresented in consumer satisfaction
surveys because of lower educational attainment and difficulties
with functional abilities such as seeing and writing. Seltzer (1981)
addressed these concerns accordingly:

> Perhaps if satisfaction is defined more broadly to include cli-
> ents' affective responses to interactions and situations, then
> additional nonverbal means will be developed to investigate
> this important domain of community adjustment. (p. 629)

High degrees of consumer satisfaction may also be related to
recipients' fears that the service may be discontinued if one is too
critical. There may be a belief that any service is better than no
service, that is, *I'm more satisfied having the service than not having it, regardless of quality.* In their report on a Consumer Satisfaction Survey conducted in the state of Colorado, Sands, Kozleski,

and Goodwin (1991) examined the issue of high reported satisfaction:

> On the other hand, it could be interpreted that the degree of satisfaction is linked to participants who may have been enculturated by a service delivery system that has the potential to create a sense of dependency and compliance. That is, whatever a service recipient gets is satisfactory since it is better than not getting service. (p. 312)

Social factors may also unduly influence the response of individuals who have developmental disabilities. Corey, Corey, and Callanan (1993) suggested that consumers of human services generally hold a positive attitude about "helping" professions and individuals who provide these services. This attitude may intensify the proclivity of individuals with developmental disabilities to acquiesce by "responding affirmatively to questions regardless of their content" (Sigelman, Budd, Spanhel, & Schoenrock, 1981, p. 53).

THE GEORGIA CONSUMER SATISFACTION SURVEY

The 1987 Amendments to the Developmental Disabilities Assistance and Bill of Rights Act required each State Developmental Disabilities Planning Council to conduct a comprehensive review and analysis of satisfaction with various services provided to people with developmental disabilities. Data gathered for the Georgia Council on Developmental Disabilities Consumer Satisfaction Survey Project (Leedy & Keller, 1989) are highlighted in the following paragraphs. These data should be examined in light of the aforementioned concerns.

Satisfaction with services received ranged from sixty-nine percent (69%) to one-hundred percent (100%). Some consumers indicated dissatisfaction with programs and services where therapy or direct services were being provided such as rehabilitation services and education. Reasons for dissatisfaction were primarily because of the manner in which services were delivered, lack of individualized services, lack of trained professionals, lack of knowledge about how to access services, and limited supply.

It is important to note that substantial numbers of respondents did not receive the services in question. For example, eighty-seven percent (87%) of respondents reported that they were satisfied or very satisfied with transportation to and from work. However, only 160 of 400 consumers (40%) reported that they worked or used transportation to and from work. Furthermore, consumers indicated that they were not satisfied with transportation for non-daily activities, weekday leisure, and weekend leisure activities.

Various data had specific implications for leisure service providers. For example:

- Seventy-five percent (75%) of respondents were satisfied with life in general. Consumer comments indicated life satisfaction was contingent upon quality of work status, relationships with people, and involvement in leisure.
- Seventy percent (70%) were satisfied with how they spent their spare time. Consumers stated, however, that they would like more after-school and weekend activity, more social contacts, and would like to go out more.
- Eighty-seven percent of respondents (87%) were satisfied with recreation and leisure services. The consumers who were dissatisfied felt there were not enough services, or that they were not appropriate. The dissatisfied consumers wanted more swimming, exercise, bowling, sports, clubs and groups, and more Special Olympics activities.

RECOMMENDATIONS FOR THE FUTURE

How should service providers and researchers seek and interpret consumer satisfaction data without presenting an overly optimistic view of the service system? The following suggestions are offered for consideration.

Analysts should seek and listen to the voices of consumers, being careful to ask the "why" questions and not just the "what" or "how" questions. There must be an awareness of the many ways in which these voices may be heard, such as through interviews (Malik, Ashton-Shaeffer, & Kleiber, 1991), informal conversations, participant observation, or, sometimes, unexplained personality or behavior changes, particularly during times of transition, such as from school to work or work to retirement. Wadsworth and Harper (1991) presented a model for interviewing adults with moderate to severe mental retardation. They used picture cues to ask the participants about where they lived and how they felt they were treated by the staff. The success of their method suggested that the forty-seven adults were the best judges of their own living situations and quality of life, and that they could provide reliable information about their "moods, thoughts, preferences, and living environments when questions are presented in a structured and supported format" (Wadsworth & Harper, 1991, p. 228).

Investigators should employ triangulation of data using multiple data sources and types of data to draw conclusions. For example, a study might include the public forums and focus groups that were used in the Georgia Consumer Satisfaction Survey, as well as mail surveys, and face-to-face interviews. Videotaping may be used to discover nuances of meaning in verbal and nonverbal expression (Taylor & Bogdan, 1994). Documents such as photographs and personal collections/possessions may illuminate, and sometimes alter, interpretations of consumer satisfaction (Taylor & Bogdan, 1994).

Investigators may examine differences in satisfaction by disability groups. Data from the Georgia Consumer Satisfaction Survey (Leedy & Keller, 1989) indicated that consumer needs varied. For example, individuals with cognitive disabilities were more likely to express a need for educational services and resources, while consumers with orthopedic disabilities expressed needs for adaptive equipment and personal care assistance. Sample questions could explore whether individuals with cognitive disabilities report higher levels of satisfaction or different perceived needs than individuals with physical, sensory, or emotional disabilities.

Differences in satisfaction by age groups may also be examined. Roberts (1992) pointed out that the current cohort of older adults with developmental disabilities was never given the opportunity to exercise choice. However, these consumers have a unique contribution to make because of their historical perspective on services (Pederson, Chaikin, Koehler, Campbell, & Arcand, 1993). There may be cohort or generational differences in expectations, and thus satisfaction with services or perceptions of need.

Service providers and researchers should also look outside the circle of known recipients and examine comparison groups of nonrecipients. Who are they? Why do they not utilize services? Is there a discrepancy between needs perceptions of older adults with developmental disabilities and the quantity and quality of provided services?

CONCLUSION

The approach to determining consumer satisfaction advocated in this paper is based upon the belief that older adults with developmental disabilities can participate and speak for themselves, and can provide useful information pertaining to service issues. Researchers and service providers should recognize the valuable contribution older adults can offer because of their lifelong perspective. By listening closely to their voices, and being responsive to the various ways in which they may be heard, meaningful consumer satisfaction data may be obtained. This will in turn lead to a higher quality of service provision.

AUTHOR NOTE

Dr. Wilhite is interested in leisure across the lifespan with a focus on late life transitions and community inclusion. A major area reflected in her teaching, service, and research activities is the need for nontraditional approaches to reach underserved and isolated older adults. This interest is demonstrated in her work pertaining to leisure and older adults with developmental disabilities, home-centered frail elderly, and older adults living in rural enviroments.

Ms. Sheldon's current research interest is the effect of acquired urinary incontinence on leisure behavior of adult women. Prior to beginning her studies at UGA, Ms. Sheldon was a Senior Center director for 5 years in her hometown of Ellensburg, WA. For her master's thesis at Central Washington University she surveyed every senior center in the state of Washington to learn the degree to which older adults with mental retardation were participating in, and welcomed to, senior center programs.

REFERENCES

Berger, M. (1983). Toward maximizing the utility of consumer satisfaction as an outcome. In M. Lambert, E. Christensen, & S. DeJulio, *The assessment of psychotherapy outcome.* New York: Wiley.

Corey, G., Corey, M. S., & Callanan, P. (1993). *Issues and ethics in the helping professions* (4th ed.). Pacific Grove, CA: Brooks/Cole.

Developmental Disabilities Assistance and Bill of Rights Act as amended by the Developmental Disabilities Assistance and Bill of Rights Act of 1987, Public Law 100-146.

Dillman, D. A. (1978). *Mail and telephone surveys: The total design method.* New York: John Wiley & Sons.

Leedy, C. A., & Keller, M. J. (1989). *1990 Developmental disabilities report: Project B, consumer satisfaction.* Atlanta, GA: Governor's Council on Developmental Disabilities.

Little, V. C. (1982). *Open care for the aging: Comparative international approaches.* New York: Springer.

Malik, P. B., Ashton-Shaeffer, C., & Kleiber, D. A. (1991). Interviewing young adults with mental retardation: A seldom used research method. *Therapeutic Recreation Journal, 25*(1), 60-73.

Morris, R., & Harris, E. (1972). Home health services in Massachusetts, 1974: Their role in care of the long-term sick. *American Journal of Public Health, 62*(8), 1088-1092.

Pederson, E. L., Chaikin, M., Campbell, A., & Arcand, M. (1993). Strategies that close the gap between research, planning, and self-advocacy. In E. Sutton, A. R. Factor, B. A. Hawkins, T. Heller, & G. B. Seltzer (Eds.), *Older adults with developmental disabilities: Optimizing choice and change* (pp. 277-313). Baltimore, MD: Brookes.

Roberts, R. S. (1992, October). Enriching later-life experiences of older adults with developmental disabilities. In *Leisure and older adults with developmental disabilities: Issues, problems, and practice.* Symposium conducted at the meeting of the National Recreation and Park Association/National Therapeutic Recreation Society Institute, Cincinnati, OH.

Sands, D. J., Kozleski, E. B., & Goodwin, L. D. (1991). Whose needs are we meeting? Results of a consumer satisfaction survey of persons with developmental disabilities in Colorado. *Research in Developmental Disabilities, 12,* 297-314.

Seltzer, G. B. (1981). Community residential adjustment: The relationship among environment, performance, and satisfaction. *American Journal of Mental Deficiency, 85*(6), 624-630.

Sigelman, C. K., Budd, E. C., Spanhel, C. L., & Schoenrock, C. J. (1981). When in doubt, say yes: Acquiescence in interviews with mentally retarded persons. *Mental Retardation, 19*(2), 53-58.

Taylor, S. J., & Bogdan, R. (1994). Qualitative research methods and community living. In M. F. Hayden, & B. H. Abery (Eds.), *Challenges for a service system in transition: Ensuring quality community experiences for persons with developmental disabilities* (pp. 43-63). Baltimore, MD: Brookes.

Wadsworth, J. S., & Harper, D. C. (1991). Increasing the reliability of self-report by adults with moderate mental retardation. *Journal of the Association for Persons with Severe Handicaps, 16*(4), 228-232.

Chapter 7

Integration and Leisure Education for Older Adults with Developmental Disabilities

Gail Hoge
Barbara Wilhite

SUMMARY. As the population of older adults with developmental disabilities increases, these individuals experience a variety of changes and transitions. Maintaining a high quality of life during these changes and transitions is a critical issue for older adults with developmental disabilities, their families, and service providers. The purpose of this paper is to describe a model for integrating older adults with disabilities into community recreation and leisure opportunities. Recreation integration efforts may be difficult without accompanying leisure education, therefore, leisure education models, materials, and related programs useful in designing leisure education programs for older adults with developmental disabilities will be reviewed. *[Article copies available from The Haworth Document Delivery Service: 1-800-342-9678. E-mail address: getinfo@haworth.com]*

Gail Hoge, PhD, is Program Development Coordinator, University of Georgia University Affiliated Program for Persons with Developmental Disabilities and Adjunct Assistant Professor, Department of Recreation and Leisure Studies, University of Georgia.

Barbara Wilhite, EdD, CTRS, is Recreation Coordinator, Department of Recreation and Leisure Studies, University of North Texas.

[Haworth co-indexing entry note]: "Integration and Leisure Education for Older Adults with Developmental Disabilities." Hoge, Gail and Barbara Wilhite. Co-published simultaneously in *Activities, Adaptation & Aging* (The Haworth Press, Inc.) Vol. 21, No. 3, 1997, pp. 79-90; and: *Older Adults with Developmental Disabilities and Leisure: Issues, Policy, and Practice* (ed: Ted Tedrick) The Haworth Press, Inc., 1997, pp. 79-90. Single or multiple copies of this article are available for a fee from The Haworth Document Delivery Service [1-800-342-9678, 9:00 a.m. - 5:00 p.m. (EST). E-mail address: getinfo@haworth.com].

The population of older adults with developmental disabilities has grown significantly over the past two decades (Hawkins & Kultgen, 1991). As these individuals move into later maturity, they experience a variety of changes and transitions. For example, expanded residential options have made it possible for increased numbers of adults with developmental disabilities to live in community settings. In addition, the opportunity to retire "from" work "to" meaningful and enjoyable lives in the community is now possible. Maintaining a high quality of life is a critical issue for older adults with developmental disabilities, their families, and service providers.

Involvement in recreation and leisure is an integral part of the quality of community life. The purpose of this paper is first, to describe a model for integrating older adults with disabilities into community recreation and leisure opportunities (Keller, 1991; Wilhite, Keller, & Nicholson, 1991). Second, leisure education models, materials, and related programs useful in designing leisure education for older adults with developmental disabilities will be reviewed.

RECREATION INTEGRATION PROCESS

Recreation integration as described in this model is a process. The eight steps included in this process (see Figure 1) are discussed in the following paragraphs. Recreation integration may be difficult without accompanying leisure education for older adults with developmental disabilities. Therefore, where appropriate within the model, links to leisure education are highlighted.

The first step in the integration process is to *define the target population*. Older adults with developmental disabilities as well as professionals in recreation, aging, and disabilities need to be identified and assessed. A successful recreation integration experience can be promoted when characteristics such as needs, experiences, background, attitudes, and skills of consumers and service providers are carefully considered.

The second step in the integration process is to *discover specific recreation integration needs and interests*. As Stroud and Sutton (1988) have pointed out, it is impossible to generalize about the

FIGURE 1

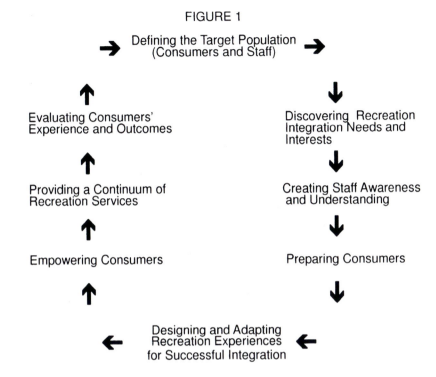

recreation activity preferences of the older population. Emphasis during this phase of the integration process should be on helping older adults explore their own recreation choices. Accordingly, self awareness in relation to leisure is a vital component in leisure education. Areas to be explored include older adults' attitudes, values, capabilities, and behaviors in relation to leisure, and the benefits they wish to obtain from integrated recreation experiences.

In steps three and four of the process, *key players must be prepared for their roles and responsibilities in facilitating community recreation integration.* Older adults with developmental disabilities, their families and friends, community members, and service providers may need to be educated about leisure and about integration. Recreation integration is not merely placing two groups together and conducting an activity (Keller, 1991). Older adults with developmental disabilities may require assistance developing the social interaction and recreation activity skills necessary to pursue the leisure choices they have identified–another key component of leisure education.

In these steps of the recreation integration process, personnel in aging, developmental disabilities, and recreation may benefit from leisure education. They must first understand and value the role of leisure in their lives before they can fully comprehend its role in the lives of older adults with developmental disabilities. They may need a more complete understanding of the recreation needs, interests, abilities, and preferences of older adults with developmental disabilities. And, they will most likely require training on how to provide a wide range of recreation activities and services, and ways to adapt or modify present activities and services so that these individuals can benefit from chosen experiences.

Some recreation experiences may need to be specifically *designed and/or adapted to facilitate successful integration,* the fifth step of the recreation integration process. Personnel must obtain input from older adults with developmental disabilities regarding the types of activities to facilitate older adults' preferred method of participation, and desired times and locations (Stroud & Sutton, 1988). In this stage of the integration process, leisure education focuses on identifying barriers and creating alternatives and modifications.

When older adults with developmental disabilities are fully involved in the process of identifying, preparing for, and participating in recreation and leisure experiences, they are *empowered.* As they become aware of personal leisure choices, older adults with developmental disabilities are motivated to seek these choices, and as they develop (or are developing, for example, through partial participation) the necessary participation skills, they are *free* or *empowered* within the context of leisure participation. This sixth step of the integration process is related to leisure education components that stress concepts such as choice, decision making, awareness of self, and competence.

As older adults with developmental disabilities begin to identify and pursue their leisure choices, it is important that an array of community participation options is available. A *continuum of recreation services,* the seventh step, provides a variety of activity choices ranging in degree of restrictiveness and integration; the least restrictive and most normalized setting possible is sought. This array of options is needed to address differing recreation and integration needs, abilities, and preferences of older adults with developmental disabilities; to promote their uniqueness; to assist them in becoming the best that they can be during leisure; and to allow them to exercise choice. The concept of choice becomes less potent in the absence of a variety or continuum of meaningful participation options. As part of leisure education, providers must help older adults with developmental disabilities become aware of these options, facilitate their choice making and participation, and help them evaluate the results of their participation.

Certainly in any effort that enables older adults with developmental disabilities to identify and pursue leisure choices, it is important to constantly seek feedback or *evaluation* of experiences and outcomes. In the eighth and final step of the integration process, all of the participants previously identified—older adults with developmental disabilities, agency personnel, family members and friends, community members—should have opportunities to evaluate and provide feedback. Evaluation and revision may occur in any of the phases of the process that have been discussed. As a result of this type of input, appropriate changes are initiated. In leisure education, older adults with developmental disabilities are encouraged to consider their recreation and leisure participation and determine how it may change over time.

LEISURE EDUCATION MODELS, MATERIALS, AND RELATED PROGRAMS

The successful integration of older adults into community recreation and leisure opportunities will be enhanced by leisure education curricula specifically designed to address their needs. The following paragraphs review leisure education models, materials, and other related programs useful to professionals interested in designing leisure education programs for older adults with developmental disabilities.

Three leisure education models have been developed specifically for people with developmental disabilities (Joswiak, 1989; Beck-Ford & Brown, 1984; and The Center for Recreation and Disability

Studies, 1991). While these appear to have been developed with younger people in mind, they can be adapted for use with older adults. These three models will be reviewed in greater detail.

Joswiak's model (1989) emphasizes awareness of leisure resources in the home and community. It features a systems approach to program design and includes terminal performance objectives, enabling objectives, and performance measures. The program contains eighteen leisure education sessions intended to be conducted two times per week for nine weeks. Most sessions are designed to last about thirty minutes to one hour in length depending on the size of the group, ability levels, focus, and interest.

Joswiak recommends and includes systematic assessment procedures that are designed to help evaluate the effectiveness of the program. These include objective and subjective assessment of participants' attainment of objectives. Pre-assessment involves interviewing participants on each enabling objective as well as assessing their participation in leisure activities. Post assessment can occur after each session or during subsequent sessions. Facilitators simply make note of which enabling objectives have been reached. Once the entire program is complete participants are reassessed using the Participation in Leisure Activities assessment sheet.

Joswiak's program is very detailed, providing the lecture content and activities for each leisure education session. The three terminal objectives for the program incorporate important areas of leisure involvement: (1) the meaning of play and leisure; (2) leisure resources in the home; and (3) leisure resources in the community. It would be possible to develop additional units related to retirement and use of senior centers for this model. Joswiak also includes helpful techniques and strategies for conducting the individual sessions, creating resources such as a leisure bulletin board, structuring the home environment to encourage leisure participation, and adapting the model for day programs.

Beck-Ford and Brown (1984) also developed a leisure education curriculum for people with developmental disabilities. Their model includes the five components of awareness of self, awareness of leisure, decision making, social interaction, and leisure and related skills (Mundy & Odum, 1979). The model incorporates Nash's (1960) ideas about the hierarchy of recreation activities. Nash suggested that some activities are more readily participated in than others because they require less self-investment, organization, or personal interaction. Accordingly, Beck-Ford and Brown categorized activities into four levels ranging from spectator (low) to creative activities (high).

This model also uses a systems approach and has a developmental sequence of learning activities. As the program is delivered, corresponding changes occur in the role of the leader from director to observer, and in the role and expectations of the client from commitment and participation in the program to commitment to initiate and participate. Changes also occur in the progression of activities from simple to complex, in the training schedule from one that is more structured to flexible, and in the instructional approach from authoritative to participatory.

There are four sections for each level (spectator to creative) in the Beck-Ford and Brown model. Section one, an introduction, includes a discussion of how to approach training, general content related to leisure awareness, self-awareness, decision making, social interaction, and leisure and allied skills. Section two lists specific objectives for each component area. Section three presents assessments related to the objectives. Included are an assessment summary sheet, a target worksheet for primary and secondary objectives to be covered in the training, and a lesson plan worksheet. Section four includes strategies and specific activities the leisure educator can use in each lesson. In using this model the service provider would assess participants, determine which objectives were most appropriate, and design lessons using the strategies provided. The appendices include a comprehensive assessment, a sample all-day inservice on leisure education, and two sample lesson plans for each level.

The Wake Leisure Education Model (The Center for Recreation and Disabilities Studies, 1991) was designed to be used in high schools to prepare students with developmental disabilities for transition to community life. The curriculum stresses the important themes of choice, independence, planning, and barriers. The model contains ten lessons, each of which may require one or two hour sessions depending on the participants. The units contain five parts: (1) goals; (2) objectives; (3) session outline; (4) materials needed;

and (5) suggestions. All materials (e.g., activities and exercises) are included in the training package. An important focus of this model is parent involvement including a family questionnaire and a guide to students' leisure notebooks.

Several other resources will prove useful to professionals developing leisure education for older adults with developmental disabilities. These include a second leisure education model developed by the Center for Recreation and Disability Studies (1989), a leisure education text authored by Dattilo and Murphy (1991), and a manual developed for use by service providers to acquaint older adults with leisure habits and lifestyles that promote health and well-being (Keller, McCombs, Pilgrim, & Booth, 1987).

The Community Reintegration Program model (The Center for Recreation and Disabilities Studies, 1989) was developed and tested through a grant from the Rehabilitation Services Administration. The program was developed to respond to the needs of adults leaving rehabilitation hospitals and returning to their communities. The twelve units comprising the program are designed to be completed in one or two sessions. The units are organized by objectives with descriptions of strategies to facilitate achievement of objectives. In this model, a therapeutic recreation specialist works closely with participants. However, the program can also be used as a self-instructional package.

Participants receive a manual which includes activities to complete as they move through the program. Unit topics include: (1) what you do for recreation; (2) why you do it; (3) how it's done; (4) can you do it now; (5) ways to make it happen; (6) barriers; (7) making plans; (8) what else is there; and (9) resources. The last session is used to help participants reevaluate and revise recreation participation goals, and articulate plans for reintegration in the community.

Dattilo's and Murphy's (1991) leisure education text contains a wealth of information regarding developing leisure education curricula. The text has three main sections. Section A provides an overview of leisure education, background in the theoretical underpinnings of leisure education, suggested areas of content for leisure education, tips on how to present leisure education, and procedures for adapting programs. Of particular usefulness are the specific leisure education program components found in Section B. Six leisure education programs with goals, objectives and performance measures, as well as the content and process of lessons, orientation activities, learning activities, discussions, and debriefings, are provided. The components included are leisure appreciation, awareness of self in leisure, self-determination in leisure, making decisions regarding leisure participation, knowledge and utilization of resources, facilitating leisure, and social interaction. Finally, Section C, a major portion of the book, is devoted to specific leisure education program activities such as: (1) swimming; (2) walking; (3) gardening; (4) bowling; (5) softball; and (6) volleyball. These are actual skill building lessons that incorporate components of leisure education.

Though not a comprehensive leisure education model, the manual developed by Keller et al. (1987) would be helpful to those designing leisure education curricula for older adults with developmental disabilities. The manual contains six steps service providers can implement with individuals or groups. These are: (1) discovering leisure time activities and interests; (2) exploring leisure interests; (3) selecting a leisure activity; (4) beginning the leisure activity; (5) checking on participant progress; and (6) investigating additional leisure pursuits. Sample activity forms and exercises are included such as a time diary, leisure interest inventory, and leisure preferences exercise. Keller et al. also encourages the building of a resource file and includes a format for creating resource cards. The final appendix is an "activity prescription" participants can write for themselves to create commitment.

No one planning leisure education programs should be without two excellent resources developed by Stumbo (1992) and Stumbo and Thompson (1986). Both resources include a host of different activities to use with groups and individuals in leisure education. The majority of activities are of the pencil and paper response type which may need to be adapted to accommodate the needs and abilities of older adults with developmental disabilities. The activities and exercises in these resources provide a method of enhancing the different components of a leisure education curricula.

An additional resource for developing leisure education curricula for older adults with developmental disabilities is a unit on leisure and recreation found in Cotten et al.'s pre-retirement training manual

(1991) for older adults with developmental disabilities. The manual has an accompanying participant workbook.

Each chapter in the manual contains goals and objectives, teaching methods, activities for participants, resources needed, and lesson plans. The section on leisure and recreation focuses on activity and hobby options and preferences, understanding the benefits of participation in activities and hobbies, equipment needed to participate in activities, local organizations that provide opportunities to participate in recreation, and practicing social skills that are relevant to leisure activity participation. Cotten uses pictures of actual people participating in recreation activities for this section. For example, in unit one, participants are presented a group of eighty-one pictures of activities and choose five they prefer. The last unit focuses on social behaviors including acceptable dress applicable to social situations, understanding differences in individual versus group activities, and types of relationships. Again, the pictures are used to reinforce learning about these concepts. Some of the activities included in Cotten's manual could be adapted for use in leisure education curriculum for older adults with developmental disabilities.

Finally, two additional resources may also be helpful when designing leisure education programs for older adults with developmental disabilities. The text and accompanying handbook developed by Stroud and Sutton (1988) have many useful suggestions applicable to leisure education programs. The text has valuable information and suggestions for working with older adults with developmental disabilities. The handbook provides some excellent leisure education topics and activities. For example, appearance and cleanliness, making small talk, meeting new people, getting to know the community, available services and activities (senior centers), using public transportation, and of course, specific leisure and recreation activities. Examples of some of the activities included are hobbies, gardening, keeping a pet, and visiting a museum. All of the activities are age appropriate and comprehensive.

CONCLUSION

As the population of older adults with developmental disabilities expands and moves into community settings, their participation in community programs will grow as well. It is imperative to prepare them for meaningful involvement in recreation and leisure pursuits. To insure integrated recreation and leisure opportunities, therapeutic recreation specialists and other service professionals will need to carefully plan inclusion efforts, and design leisure education curricula to address the needs of older adults with developmental disabilities. Acceptance and implementation of inclusive recreation and leisure programs will not be without challenges. However, the recreation integration model presented provides a strategy for professionals designing such programs. Additionally, the leisure education models, materials, and programs highlighted will be invaluable in developing programs that prepare older adults with developmental disabilities for meaningful leisure and recreation participation; each has something to offer. By adding or subtracting components, or making adaptations to activities to suit the needs and abilities of older adults with developmental disabilities, they can provide a base for developing a leisure education curriculum for aging participants with developmental disabilities.

AUTHOR NOTE

Dr. Hoge is responsible for working collaboratively with the faculty and staff of the UAP to identify and develop innovative programmatic initiatives and to secure funding to support these initiatives, developing and implementing the evaluation plan of the UAP, and participating in pre-service and in-service training activities. She is currently project advisor on the Georgia PAS Corps, an AmeriCorps project providing personal assistance service to people with disabilities. She was co-principal investigator on a field initiated research project titled "Project TRAIL (Transition through Recreation and Integration for Life)" funded by the Department of Education, NIDRR. She directed an Administration on Developmental Disabilities Project of National Significance titled, "Enhancement of Minority Participation in Developmental Disabilities Initiative."

Dr. Hoge is a certified therapeutic recreation specialist. She completed BS and MS degrees in therapeutic recreation at Florida State University, Tallahassee, FL and the doctorate in Human Performance and Leisure Behavior at Indiana University, Bloomington.

Dr. Wilhite is interested in leisure across the lifespan with a focus on late life transitions and community inclusion. A major area reflected in her teaching, service, and research activities is the need for nontraditional approaches to reach underserved and isolated older adults. This interest is demonstrated in her work pertaining to leisure and older adults with developmental disabilities, home-centered frail elderly, and older adults living in rural environments.

REFERENCES

Beck-Ford, V., & Brown, R. (1984). *Leisure training and rehabilitation.* Springfield, IL: Charles C Thomas.

Cotten, P. D., Casey, J., Laughlin, C. Gardner, M., & Britt, C. R. (1991). *Pre-Retirement Assessment and Planning for Older Adults with Mental Retardation.* Sanatorium, MS: Boswell Retardation Center.

Dattilo, J., & Murphy, W. D. (1991). *Leisure education program planning: A systematic approach.* State College, PA: Venture Publishing, Inc.

Joswiak, K. F. (1989). *Leisure education: Program materials for persons with developmental disabilities.* State College, PA: Venture Publishing, Inc.

Keller, M. J. (1991). Creating a recreation integration process among older adults with mental retardation. *Educational Gerontology,* 17, 275-288.

Keller, M. J., McCombs, J., Pilgrim, V. C., & Booth, S. A. (1987). *Helping older adults develop active leisure lifestyles.* Athens, GA: The University of Georgia, Institute of Community and Area Development.

Mundy, J., & Odum, L. (1979). *Leisure education: Theory and practice.* New York, NY: John Wiley and Sons.

Nash, J. B (1960). *Philosophy of recreation and leisure.* Dubuque, IA: William C. Brown.

Peterson, C. A., & Gunn, S. L. (1984). *Therapeutic recreation program design* (2nd ed.). Englewood Cliffs, NJ: Prentice-Hall, Inc.

Stumbo, N. J. (1992). *Leisure education II: More activities and resources.* State College, PA: Venture Publishing, Inc.

Stumbo, N. J., & Thompson, S. R. (1986). *Leisure education: A manual of activities and resources.* State College, PA: Venture Publishing, Inc.

Stroud, M., & Sutton, E. (1988). *Activities Handbook and Instructor's Guide.* Baltimore: Brookes Publishing.

Stroud, M., & Sutton, E. (1988). *Expanding Options for Older Adults with Developmental Disabilities* Baltimore: Brookes Publishing.

The Center for Recreation and Disability Studies. (1989). *The community reintegration program.* Chapel Hill, NC: The University of North Carolina at Chapel Hill, Curriculum in Leisure Studies and Recreation Administration.

The Center for Recreation and Disability Studies. (1991) *The Wake leisure education program: An integral part of special education.* Chapel Hill, NC: The University of North Carolina at Chapel Hill, Curriculum in Leisure Studies and Recreation Administration.

Wilhite, B., Keller, M. J., & Nicholson, L. (1991). Integrating older persons with developmental disabilities into community recreation: Theory and practice. *Activities, Adaptation & Aging,* 15(1/2), 111-129.

Chapter 8

Issues Resolved and Unresolved: A Look to the Future

Ted Tedrick

"Issues resolved" in the title is perhaps an inaccurate descriptor as much of what is presented in this monograph more accurately represents a transition, rather than a finite closure when previous concerns are viewed. Progress has been made on many fronts when leisure pertaining to an older population with developmental disabilities is considered; as examples: model programs continue to be implemented, evaluated, and reported; contact between aging services professionals and the MR/DD network proceeds with the goal of better serving clients, although not as quickly or comprehensively as desired, and researchers are exploring questions of both a basic and applied nature. The aging of adults with developmental disabilities is no longer invisible to the public.

Comments in the introduction spoke of the need to revisit issues presented in an earlier, edited volume (Keller, 1991, *Activities with Developmentally Disabled Elderly and Older Adults*). Topics in the 1991 monograph are similar to many areas addressed in this collection of manuscripts. Models of program delivery were presented

Ted Tedrick, PhD, is Professor, Department of Sport Management and Leisure Studies, Temple University.

[Haworth co-indexing entry note]: "Issues Resolved and Unresolved: A Look to the Future." Tedrick, Ted. Co-published simultaneously in *Activities, Adaptation & Aging* (The Haworth Press, Inc.) Vol. 21, No. 3, 1997, pp. 91-103; and: *Older Adults with Developmental Disabilities and Leisure: Issues, Policy, and Practice* (ed: Ted Tedrick) The Haworth Press, Inc., 1997, pp. 91-103. Single or multiple copies of this article are available for a fee from The Haworth Document Delivery Service [1-800-342-9678, 9:00 a.m. - 5:00 p.m. (EST). E-mail address: getinfo@haworth.com].

(Carter & Foret, 1991; Riddick & Keller, 1991), interventions focused on the arts (Edelson, 1991; Harlan, 1991), expressive therapies were described (Segal, 1991), and integration of elders with mental retardation into community settings and activities was a theme, as well (Wilhite, Keller & Nicholson, 1991; Zimpel, 1991). Similarly, authors herein have described innovative interventions in the arts (Barret & Clements, chapter four), fitness programming (Hawkins, chapter two; Frizzell, chapter three), and the need for community integration of this population (Hoge & Wilhite, chapter seven). It can be assumed that earlier work has paved the way for continued development of programs and models; Hoge and Wilhite (chapter seven), as examples, refer to Keller's (1991) integration model and Joswiak's (1989) approach to leisure education. Likewise, Hawkin's (1993) research has established the foundation for advocating active leisure programming through her reporting of the link between leisure involvement and life satisfaction in older adults with mental retardation. Thus, the notion of "transitioning" is appropriate; we continue to forge ahead using the work of those dedicated to improving services for and lives of this group.

Among the unresolved issues are the negative perceptions held by aging adults with MR/DD toward retirement and the lack of pre-retirement preparation programs to assist those contemplating a cessation of work and a move into a life phase where leisure, rather than paid employment, offers the basis for daily living and life satisfaction. Linked to retirement is the concept of leisure and the freedom it affords. With freedom comes choice and choices made may not be those best-suited to healthy living or personal development. Thus, leisure education which includes decision making skills should be promoted as a component of pre-retirement planning and preparation.

The training or cross-training (involving staff from both the MR/DD and aging systems) of staff who work with adults having developmental disabilities is another pressing issue. Concerns such as who should provide and attend such training, what content areas need to be covered, and what outcomes must be reached are examined. The final topic presented is that of research: where we are currently, what questions are pertinent, and suggested methodologies focus the presentation in this final section.

RETIREMENT

Retirement as a meaningful concept for aging adults with MR/ DD must be viewed as an institution in its infancy and one which may differ in fundamental ways from the post-employment experiences of non-developmentally disabled older adults. Retirement for this latter group may be linked with a comfortable home setting with ownership assured through the burning of the mortgage, a spouse and children/grandchildren within reasonable distance, a variety of interesting activities from which to select, many around the home and others of a formal nature within the community, and perhaps a work history of 40 or more years which had culminated in some type of recognition for a job well done. Retirement is an expected event, most frequently planned for to some degree, and financed through a pension plan.

Life histories for many adults in their 40s, 50s, or 60s having developmental disabilities differ markedly from the scenario above. Sutton (chapter five) notes the effects of deinstitutionalization in the 1970s on the lives of today's cohort of middle-aged and older adults with MR/DD—community placements, training, and sheltered workshops were the norm for most. The degree to which free time options are available or encouraged in group living sites, the lack of access to normalized, integrated community programs such as senior centers, and the experience or inexperience with making decisions all shape what retirement may mean for adults with developmental disabilities. It is understandable that professionals have argued against retirement for this population (Blaney, 1990) and that older adults with MR/DD themselves are fearful and wish to continue working (Stroud, Roberts, & Murphy, 1986)—what lies on the other side may be unstructured, rather nebulous, and limited, especially when contrasted with the security of the job which society values greatly and the friends and routine provided by paid work. Thus, application of the traditional concept of retirement may be inappropriate. Blaney's (1990) point that goals, objectives, and agency-mandated outcomes may run counter to the essence of retirement—freedom and intrinsic motivation—is well taken.

Perhaps the solution begins with a concept as described by Sutton, Sterns, and Schwartz-Park (1993, p. 98):

Pragmatically, the MR/DD system as it exists indicates that alternative-to-work programming (retirement programs) is realistic and necessary. The use of time is a classic issue of immense importance to the general population and not unique to people with developmental disabilities. The trend is toward providing a wide range of work and leisure options for later life and giving individuals the information they need to make good choices.

Options and information needed to make good choices are keys, it would seem, to a successful work-retirement transition in mature adulthood. As revealed in a survey by Sutton and colleagues, much more needs to be done to adequately prepare adults with MR/DD for possible retirement and positive alternatives to work must go beyond passively viewing television programs in group homes or other sites. It was found that about half the adults (55+) were working full time and 41% were in some type of work alternative (retirement) program. About 1/3 of responding sites offered full-time recreation programs and more than half offered part-time activities for older adults. In terms of preparation about one-half of the sites offered nothing to ready older adults for retirement. Also of interest was the finding that fewer than 1 in 10 adults (55+) with MR/DD were using community-based adult day care services (Sutton, Sterns, & Schwartz-Park, 1983). Notable, as well, is the fact that Ohio (the survey site) is a state that by law allows adults with MR/DD to retire; states without such legislation would be expected to be doing less in terms of preretirement and retirement activities. When Factor (1993) analyzed the involvement of state MR/DD agencies in discrete initiatives for their aging adults, only 10 states were shown to be substantively involved in such initiatives. Thus, if the information we are gaining from the more progressive states indicates that meager pre-retirement opportunities exist and that alternative-to-work programming could be vastly improved, then the need for progress on a nationwide scale is indeed significant.

Training/Cross-Training Issues

Whether the source stems from professionals within the field who recognize gaps or inadequacies in their backgrounds or from surveys which have been conducted to analyze training or cross training (having service personnel from both areas, aging and MR/DD systems, present to share concerns and experiences) needs (Kultgen and Rominger, 1993), there is an awareness that the growth of the aging population of developmentally disabled adults has proceeded faster than our ability to train large numbers of staff knowledgeable in both aging and developmental disabilities. Clients, themselves, have recognized the problem. As noted in chapter six, Wilhite and Sheldon reference a survey conducted in Georgia to ascertain consumer satisfaction. A lack of trained professionals was among the top five reasons given for dissatisfaction.

Competencies in aging and developmental disabilities are crucial in the provision of programs to individual clients and they extend to service delivery issues as each system operates differently. The following questions focus the discussion in succeeding paragraphs: For whom should training/cross training be targeted? What are the skills needed by those involved in training and where are they to be found? What approaches might be taken at the university level to prepare students with knowledge and experiences in leisure programming, developmental disabilities, and aging; and how should the topic of leisure be integrated into training efforts?

Kultgen and Rominger (1993) provide a model for cross training which divides the potential audience into two levels: administrators, policy-makers, and those affecting or developing legislation or regulations operate at the systems impact level; at the program impact level are those who provide direct services–case workers, group home staff, activity personnel, recreation therapists, etc. At the systems level it is imperative that each understands how the other's system operates. Management personnel in the mental retardation/developmental disabilities system should understand appropriate aging entitlement programs, how a continuum of service is delivered, differences in objectives of service center programs versus adult day care options and how inclusion of older adults with developmental disabilities into existing aging settings is viewed by those in the aging system. Likewise, aging systems managers must gain an awareness of programs offered through state and local MR/DD offices; crucial here is the consideration of adulthood, moving toward older adulthood, and how this factor impacts areas such as sheltered work programs, possible retirement, and training goals in life skills, etc. Obviously, the consideration of retirement and the options available when work ceases are issues pertinent to both groups of administrators.

Those involved in direct service provision operate at the program impact level. Clients are trained, supervised or assisted in a face-to-face manner and staff need knowledge about developmental disabilities and how the aging process interacts with specific disabilities. Gerontologists can provide workshops focusing on the biological, psychological, and social changes brought about by aging. Staff working in senior centers or other components of the aging network may have had little exposure to adults with mental retardation; training in the variety of developmental disabilities, typical behaviors, communication techniques and case management approaches would assist aging staff who would be involved in a community integration effort. In one survey (Rominger, Mash, & Kultgen, 1990) training in creative leisure activities ranked in the top five along with medical concerns, assessing individual service needs, age-related changes, and age-appropriate planning as topics for training by staff working with those having developmental disabilities; leisure activities ranked in the bottom quarter for those involved in the aging system. Priorities for them were medical concerns, managing life transitions, issues in mental retardation and mental illness, and working with families. Similar surveys to establish content areas of workshops should be conducted when cross-training is offered.

Experts with a background and education in both aging and developmental disabilities who might be called upon to instruct or facilitate workshops are few. One source would be University Affiliated Programs; authors in this text such as Drs. Hawkins, Wilhite and Clemments, and Boyd, are associated with UAPs at Universities of Indiana, Georgia, and Temple, respectively. It is more common to find consultants or trainers with expertise in either aging/gerontology or MR/DD. Hopefully the future will bring greater cross-over as both systems engage in training together. Having both groups in the same room creates a fertile environment where sharing can occur. Certainly more materials are being disseminated. Pederson (1993) notes the research and training consortium consisting of university programs in the midwest (Kentucky, Ohio, Indiana, Illinois, Wisconsin, and Minnesota); its purpose is to conduct research and develop training materials to be used in the field. All of the above efforts should increase the numbers of staff, teachers, and researchers competent in the combined areas of aging and developmental disabilities.

Another target group for training is university students, both undergraduate and graduate level, who may have a primary interest in either mental retardation or gerontology. Training here, labelled the "pre-service level" by Kultgen and Rominger (1993), frequently takes an interdisciplinary approach where a professor with the guidance of a group of interested faculty will structure a course focusing on demographics, services and systems, the aging process and other topics mentioned in previous paragraphs. A lead instructor may arrange guest lectures from those in the academic community and from the field. How best to reach such potential students is a question that should be analyzed at each campus. Greater interest may be seen from majors dealing with mental retardation such as social work, education, or a variety of therapies (music, art, recreation, etc.); one benefit in reaching a potential audience from the gerontology perspective is that many programs are interdisciplinary by design and collaborative efforts are already commonplace.

A special concern here is that leisure must be incorporated into such curricula. It is imperative that recreation and leisure studies faculty be involved in joint planning and instructional efforts. Increasingly the literature is revealing leisure desires, barriers, and patterns of the sub-population of aging adults with developmental disabilities. Innovative programs and demonstration projects similar to those in this monograph are in operation and are being reported at professional gatherings and in journals or books.

Noted above is the finding that creative leisure activity is an area among the top priorities for training as viewed by field staff. Staff want to know the kinds of activities which are appropriate and how to implement them. Leisure education can be delivered in an individual or group fashion. Hoge and Wilhite review model approaches in chapter seven and excellent materials exist (for example, Dattilo & Murphy, 1991; Joswiak, 1989; and Beck-Ford & Brown, 1984). Likewise, integration of older adults with MR/DD into community experiences is a consideration which will involve careful selection of clients, training of staff, and awareness on the part of individuals or groups at centers or other locations who will be a vital part of the integration process. Apparently, much needs to be done here as a recent survey (Glausier, Whorton, & Knight, 1995) showed little preference for or actual participation in community senior centers on the part of seniors (50+) with mental retardation. This study described activity as primarily passive with many barriers in existence; lack of friends and opportunities, no transportation or personal finances, and lack of skills or awareness were among the constraints. The list of topics appropriate for training in leisure is lengthy and the goal must be to include this area as a part of workshops when staff or students attend.

Research Needs and Issues

Although greater dissemination of research and successful program practice involving older adults with MR/DD has been the trend in recent years, the questions unanswered are many. Professionalism demands that empirical investigations be undertaken to build theory and to give direction to practitioners. While applied problems and concerns are apparent and immediate, we can not neglect basic research questions related to developmental disabilities, aging, and leisure participation. In beginning a research agenda the following considerations are offered.

Leisure participation patterns, desired activities, and constraints or barriers faced by adults with MR/DD are areas where surveys have provided answers. Studies (Dattilo, 1987; Glausier, Whorton, & Knight, 1995; Hawkins, 1991, 1993; Hawkins, Eklund & Martz, 1991; Hayden, Lakin, Hill, Bruininks & Copher, 1992; and Sparrow & Mayne, 1990) have revealed a dominance of passive activities (television viewing, activities around the house, music, etc.) with a need for more physical involvement. A group of barriers similar to those of non-disabled older adults, i.e., transportation and lack of skills or friends has been noted. Eating out more often and socializing outside of their living situation are activities desired on a more frequent basis. Direction is provided here by way of the need to expand opportunities and attack problems which prevent participation.

While the above patterns apply to many older adults with MR/ DD, findings cannot be generalized to all which evidences the need to conduct more research on differing sub-groups of this population. Most samples, as is understandable, have emphasized higher-functioning adults with mental retardation who have contact with the formal service system. There is a lack of information on lower-functioning adults with mental retardation and little is known about those who have not interacted with the formal system. Many live at home cared for by parents in their late seventies or eighties who have become frail or by siblings in their fifties or beyond. What leisure opportunities are typical in this situation? Are family activities pursued? Is leisure used as a respite (taking a son/daughter to a program/event) for caregivers? These questions can be probed as we seek out specialized groups. Those with cerebral palsy are rarely included in samples; Wilhite and Sheldon (chapter six) urge us to explore differences due to cognitive deficits as contrasted with orthopedic disabilities. Hawkins (1993) reported differences between adults with Down Syndrome and those with mental retardation not connected with Down Syndrome; the point is we must be careful in generalizing based upon current research and samples and seek to expand such groups when future studies are undertaken.

A wide variety of research methodologies may complement efforts to expand groups of subjects. Survey research is the primary methodology evident; Wilhite and Sheldon (chapter six) suggest that "why" questions might be answered through a number of qualitative approaches: interviews, conversations, or observations of clients/residents noting behavioral or other changes. These methods would provide the vertical depth and contextual information which would complement information gained to date from surveys. Where communication problems exist, with severely or profoundly impaired clients, for example, observational data may substitute for focused interviews.

Single-subject designs and case studies are urged, as well. In many cases obtaining large and representative samples presents difficulties to researchers; single-subject research where a selected few clients are exposed to an innovative therapy and then tracked over a period of time noting individual change relative to outcome variables is an approach within the means of most agencies. Case studies of individuals, groups, or situations can also examine what is or isn't working and under what conditions. This method has been used in examining successful community integration models (Wilhite, Keller, & Nicholson, 1991); other areas where measurable outcomes have been achieved should be examined via case studies and reported to practitioners. Of particular interest here would be cooperative relationships among the MR/DD and aging systems or other providers who may assist in program delivery. Case studies reporting friendships, social networking and attitude changes on the part of clients, staff, or friends where older adults with developmental disabilities have been exposed to community experiences would be welcomed. Both single-subject methodology and case studies appear to be most appropriate for examining many issues pertinent here.

Participatory Action Research (PAR), as noted by Pederson, Chaikin, Koehler, Campbell and Arcand (1993), places aging consumers with MR/DD in an empowered position as research is being planned. This model of inclusion where consumers and their family members work with professional staff and researchers is person-centered and may not only assist in developing topics for investigation, but may prove helpful if any ethical concerns arise during discussion. Those most affected by decisions (for example, who is to be excluded from participation and by what means is the decision made) are in the room during planning. This writer has seen the positive outcomes of consumer participation as training workshops were planned; the voices of those affected are significant. The thrust of PAR is congruent with inclusion and integration and must be a part of creating any type of research agenda.

The final note related to aging, developmental disabilities, and leisure is to urge that a means be undertaken to obtain the views of interested researchers so that an agenda or priorities might be established. This should prove positive in many ways; there might be direct connections with funders of research projects, graduate students seeking thesis topics would benefit, and duplicated efforts could be eliminated. There are a number of committees operating in professional organizations who could take the lead here or research symposia are a national vehicle for such a priority-setting session. The research consortium of the University Affiliated Programs offers another avenue. Whatever methods are used, the need to determine and disseminate a research agenda exploring leisure for older adults with developmental disabilities is immediate.

REFERENCES

Barret, D. & Clements, C. (1996). Expressive arts programming for older adults both with and without disabilities: An opportunity for inclusion, chapter four this volume.

Beck-Ford, V., & Brown, R. (1984). *Leisure training and rehabilitation.* Springfield, IL: Charles C Thomas.

Blaney, B. (1990) *Planning a vision: A resource handbook on aging and developmental disabilities.* Cambridge, MA: Human Service Research Institute.

Carter, M. J. & Foret, C. (1991). Therapeutic recreation programming for older adults with developmental disabilities. In M. J. Keller (Ed.), *Activities with developmentally disabled elderly and older adults* (35-52). New York: The Haworth Press, Inc.

Dattilo, J. (1987). Recreation and leisure literature for individuals with mental retardation: Implications for recreation. *Therapeutic Recreation Journal,* 21(1), 9-17.

Dattilo, J., & Murphy, W. D. (1991). *Leisure education program planning: A systematic approach.* State College, PA: Venture Publishing, Inc.

Edelson, R. T. (1991). Art and crafts–not "Arts and crafts"–Alternative vocational day activities for adults who are older and mentally retarded. In M.J. Keller (Ed.), *Activities with developmentally disabled elderly and older adults* (81-98). New York: The Haworth Press, Inc.

Factor, A. (1993). Translating policy into practice. In E. Sutton, A Factor, B. Hawkins, T. Heller, & G. Seltzer (Eds.), *Older adults with developmental disabilities: Optimizing choice and change* (pp. 257-275). Baltimore: Paul H. Brookes Publishing Co.

Frizzell, L. (1996). Fitness and exercise for older adults with developmental disabilities. Chapter three this volume.

Glausier, S., Whorton, J., & Knight, H. (1995). Recreation and leisure likes/dislikes of senior citizens with mental retardation. *Activities, Adaptation & Aging,* 19(3), 43-54.

Harlan, J. E. (1991). The use of art therapy for older adults with developmental disabilities. In M. J. Keller (Ed.), *Activities with developmentally disabled elderly and older adults* (67-80). New York: The Haworth Press, Inc.

Hawkins, B. (1991). An exploration of adaptive skills and leisure activity of older adults with mental retardation. *Therapeutic Recreation Journal,* 17(4), 9-27.

Hawkins, B. A. (1993). An exploratory analysis of leisure and life satisfaction in aging adults with mental retardation. *Therapeutic Recreation Journal,* 27(2), 98-109.

Hawkins, B. (1996). Health, fitness, and quality of life for older adults with developmental disabilities. Chapter 2, this volume.

Hawkins, B., Eklund, S. & Martz, B. (1991). *Detection of decline in aging adults with developmental disabilities.* Cincinnati, OH: Rehabilitation Research and Training Center Consortium on Aging and Developmental Disabilities.

Hayden, M., Lakin, K., Hill, B., Bruininks, R., & Copher, J. (1992). Social and leisure integration of people with mental retardation in foster homes and small group homes. *Education and Training in Mental Retardation,* 27(3), 187-199.

Hoge, G., & Wilhite, B. (1996). Integration and leisure education for older adults with developmental disabilities. Chapter seven this volume.

Joswiak, K. F. (1989). *Leisure education: Program materials for persons with developmental disabilities.* State College, PA: Venture Publishing, Inc.

Keller, M. J. (Ed.) (1991). *Activities with developmentally disabled elderly and older adults.* New York: The Haworth Press, Inc.

Keller, M. J. (1991). Creating a recreation integration process among older adults with mental retardation. *Educational Gerontology,* 17, 275-288.

Kultgen, P., and Rominger, R. (1993). Cross training within the aging and developmental disabilities services systems. In E. Sutton, A. Factor, B. Hawkins, T. Heller, & G. Seltzer (Eds.) *Older adults with developmental disabilities: Optimizing choice and change* (pp. 239-256). Baltimore: Paul H. Brookes Publishing Co.

Pederson, E. (1993). The research and training consortium process. In E. Sutton, A. Factor, B. Hawkins, T. Heller, & G. Seltzer (Eds.), *Older adults with developmental disabilities: Optimizing choice and change* (pp. 345-370). Baltimore: Paul H. Brookes Publishing Co.

Pederson, E., Chaikin, D., Koehler, D., Campbell, A., & Arcand, M. (1993). Strategies that close the gap between research, planning, and self-advocacy. In E. Sutton, A. Factor, B. Hawkins, T. Heller, & G. Seltzer (Eds.), *Older adults with developmental disabilities: Optimizing choice and change* (pp. 277-326). Baltimore: Paul H. Brookes Publishing Co.

Riddick, C. C. & Keller, M. J. (1991). Developing recreation services to assist elders who are developmentally disabled. In M. J. Keller (Ed.), *Activities with developmentally disabled elderly and older adults* (19-34). New York: The Haworth Press, Inc.

Rominger, R., Mash, C., & Kultgen, P. (1990). *Planning for the 1990's: A Survey of training needs regarding older adults with developmental disabilities.* Bloomington: Indiana University Institute For The Study of Developmental Disabilities, A University Affiliated Program.

Segal, R. (1991). Helping older mentally retarded persons expand their socialization skills through the use of expressive therapies. In M. J. Keller (Ed.), *Activities with developmentally disabled elderly and older adults)* (99-110). New York: The Haworth Press, Inc.

Sparrow, W., & Mayne, S. (1990). Recreation patterns of adults with intellectual disabilities. *Therapeutic Recreation Journal,* 24(3), 45-49.

Stroud, M., Roberts, R., & Murphy, M. (1986). Life status of elderly mentally retarded/developmentally disabled persons in northeast Ohio. In J. Berg (Ed.), *Science and service in mental retardation* (pp. 317-327). London: Methuen.

Sutton, E. (1996). Enriching later life experiences for people with developmental disabilities. Chapter five this volume.

Sutton, E., Sterns, H., & Schwartz-Park, L. (1993). Realities of retirement and pre-retirement planning. In E. Sutton, A. Factor, B. Hawkins, T. Heller, & G. Seltzer (Eds.) *Older adults with developmental disabilities: Optimizing Choice and Change* (pp. 95-106). Baltimore: Paul H. Brookes Publishing Co.

Wilhite, B., Keller, M. J., & Nicholson, L. (1991). Integrating older persons with developmental disabilities into community recreation: Theory to practice. In M. J. Keller (Ed.)., *Activities with developmentally disabled elderly and older adults* (pp. 111-130). New York: The Haworth Press, Inc.

Wilhite, B. & Sheldon, K. (1996). Consumer satisfaction for individuals with developmental disabilities. Chapter six this volume.

Zimple, B. (1991). Sharing activities–The Oneida County A.R.C. Cornhill Senior Center Integration Project. In M. J. Keller (Ed.), *Activities with developmentally disabled elderly and older adults* (pp. 131-140). New York: The Haworth Press, Inc.

Haworth
DOCUMENT DELIVERY
SERVICE

This valuable service provides a single-article order form for any article from a Haworth journal.

- *Time Saving:* No running around from library to library to find a specific article.
- *Cost Effective:* All costs are kept down to a minimum.
- *Fast Delivery:* Choose from several options, including same-day FAX.
- *No Copyright Hassles:* You will be supplied by the original publisher.
- *Easy Payment:* Choose from several easy payment methods.

Open Accounts Welcome for ...
- Library Interlibrary Loan Departments
- Library Network/Consortia Wishing to Provide Single-Article Services
- Indexing/Abstracting Services with Single Article Provision Services
- Document Provision Brokers and Freelance Information Service Providers

---

MAIL or *FAX* THIS ENTIRE ORDER FORM TO:

Haworth Document Delivery Service
The Haworth Press, Inc.
10 Alice Street
Binghamton, NY 13904-1580

or FAX: 1-800-895-0582
or CALL: 1-800-342-9678
9am-5pm EST

PLEASE SEND ME PHOTOCOPIES OF THE FOLLOWING SINGLE ARTICLES:

1) Journal Title: _____

    Vol/Issue/Year: _____ Starting & Ending Pages: _____

Article Title: _____

_____

2) Journal Title: _____

    Vol/Issue/Year: _____ Starting & Ending Pages: _____

Article Title: _____

_____

3) Journal Title: _____

    Vol/Issue/Year: _____ Starting & Ending Pages: _____

Article Title: _____

_____

4) Journal Title: _____

    Vol/Issue/Year: _____ Starting & Ending Pages: _____

Article Title: _____

_____

(See other side for Costs and Payment Information)

COSTS: Please figure your cost to order quality copies of an article.

1. Set-up charge per article: $8.00
   ($8.00 × number of separate articles)   _____

2. Photocopying charge for each article:

   1-10 pages: $1.00   _____

   11-19 pages: $3.00   _____

   20-29 pages: $5.00   _____

   30+ pages: $2.00/10 pages   _____

3. Flexicover (optional): $2.00/article   _____

4. Postage & Handling: US: $1.00 for the first article/

   $.50 each additional article   _____

   Federal Express: $25.00   _____

   Outside US: $2.00 for first article/
   $.50 each additional article _____

5. Same-day FAX service: $.35 per page   _____

   GRAND TOTAL: _____

METHOD OF PAYMENT: (please check one)

❏ Check enclosed   ❏ Please ship and bill. PO # _____
(sorry we can ship and bill to bookstores only! All others must pre-pay)

❏ Charge to my credit card: ❏ Visa; ❏ MasterCard; ❏ Discover;
· ❏ American Express;

Account Number: _____ Expiration date: _____

Signature: ✗ _____

Name: _____ Institution: _____

Address: _____

_____

City: _____ State: _____ Zip: _____

Phone Number: _____ FAX Number: _____

MAIL or *FAX* THIS ENTIRE ORDER FORM TO:

Haworth Document Delivery Service	**or FAX:** 1-800-895-0582
The Haworth Press, Inc.	**or CALL:** 1-800-342-9678
10 Alice Street	9am-5pm EST)
Binghamton, NY 13904-1580	